Saint Gianna Molla
Wife, Mother, Doctor

Saint Gianna

Saint Gianna Molla
Wife, Mother, Doctor

By Pietro Molla and Elio Guerriero

TRANSLATED BY JAMES G. COLBERT

IGNATIUS PRESS   SAN FRANCISCO

Original Italian edition:
Gianna: la donna forte
La beata Gianna Beretta Molla
nel ricordo del marito
© 1995, Edizioni San Paolo, Milan

Cover photograph: Saint Gianna with children
Pierluigi (holding sunglasses) and Mariolina Molla
Cover photograph courtesy of
Society of Saint Gianna Beretta Molla
Philadelphia, Penn.
(www.gianna.org)

Cover design by Riz Boncan Marsella

CONTENTS

PART ONE

A Story of Three Generations
By Elio Guerriero

PART TWO

Blessed Gianna, My Wife
An Interview with Pietro Molla
By Elio Guerriero

PART THREE

Gianna's Virtues
By Pietro Molla

FOREWORD

Saint Gianna: A Model for Mothers

"A woman of exceptional love, an outstanding wife and mother, she gave witness in her daily life to the demanding values of the Gospel." In his homily on the occasion of her beatification, April 24, 1994, Pope John Paul II proposed Gianna Beretta Molla as a model for all mothers: "By holding up this woman as an exemplar of Christian perfection, we would like to extol all those high-spirited mothers of families who give themselves completely to their family, who suffer in giving birth, who are prepared for every labor and every kind of sacrifice, so that the best they have can be given to others."

In canonizing Gianna Beretta Molla this spring, the Church officially recognized the extraordinary sanctity of a woman who chose to live an ordinary life—as a professional and, later, as a wife and mother. Though she had once considered entering a religious order, instead she practiced medicine (receiving her medical degree in 1949, and her specialty in pediatrics in 1952). She devoted herself to caring for her patients, and her selflessness and dedication as a physician endeared her to the people. But it was not only her practice of medicine that influenced them. She regarded her profession as a mission through which she could aid and nurture both bodies and souls. The young doctor's devotion to her Catholic faith was well known in her community, and especially her instruction of young Catholic girls in their faith.

Gianna meditated long and prayerfully on God's will for her. "What is a vocation?" she wrote: "It is a gift from God—it comes from God Himself! Our concern, then, should be to know the will of God. We should enter onto the path that God wills for us, not by 'forcing the door', but when God wills and as God wills."[1] Gianna believed she was called to marriage and family life, but she waited patiently for God's will to be revealed.

Gianna Beretta did not marry until she was thirty-three years old—to an engineer ten years her senior, Pietro Molla, whose sister had earlier been a patient of the young Dr. Beretta. Letters Gianna wrote during their year-long courtship reveal her deep commitment to this new vocation. The couple married in September 1955. Several days before their wedding, Gianna wrote to Pietro, reflecting on their vocation to marriage: "With God's help and blessing, we will do all we can to make our new family a little cenacle where Jesus will reign over all our affections, desires and actions. . . . We will be working with God in His creation; in this way we can give Him children who will love Him and serve Him."

Gianna's faith and her communion with Christ were profound, and from this grace she drew deeper understanding of the dedication and self-giving love that is fundamental to Christian marriage and family life.

---

[1] *Blessed Gianna Beretta Molla: A Woman's Life* (Boston: Pauline Books, 2002), pp. 71–72.

After her marriage and even after she had children Gianna continued her medical practice, extending her gifts beyond her immediate family to the children of others. Three children, a son and two daughters, were born between 1956 and 1959, and Gianna had two miscarriages before conceiving another baby in 1961. Pietro and Gianna referred to their children as their "treasures".

In his own account of these years, Pietro Molla says that he did not object to Gianna's continuing her medical practice, because she was so deeply attached to her patients, though after she became pregnant with their fourth child, Pietro and Gianna had agreed that she would stop working outside the home after the baby was born.

Early in the pregnancy it was discovered that Gianna had a fibroma, a benign tumor, on her uterine wall. Surgery that would involve aborting the baby was suggested, but the Mollas instantly and firmly rejected this idea, and chose surgery that would remove only the tumor. Because of her medical knowledge, Gianna understood more fully than most the risks involved in this delicate surgery—both to her and to her unborn child. She insisted that the baby be protected at all costs.

The surgery successfully removed the fibroma, and the pregnancy continued, apparently normally, and the family made plans for the future in joy and hope. But all was not well, and a few days before the baby was born, Gianna realized it would be a difficult—possibly life-threatening delivery. She asked her husband to promise that if it were necessary to choose between saving her and saving the baby, he should choose the baby. "I insist", she said.

On Good Friday, Gianna entered the hospital. And a lovely, healthy baby daughter, Gianna Emanuela, was born the next day, April 21, 1962. But the mother had developed a fatal infection—septic peritonitis. (Modern antibiotics most likely would have saved her.) The inflammation caused immense suffering during her final week on earth. In the midst of her terrible pain, Gianna called to her own mother, Maria, who had died in 1942—and she prayed. As she lay dying, she repeated, "Jesus, I love you", over and over. Her agony ended on April 28—at home.

She was thirty-nine. The tiny infant, Gianna Emanuela, was exactly one week old.

The bereft Pietro was left to raise four very young children without their mother: Pierluigi, the eldest, was not yet six; Mariolina, four; Laura, nearly three; and of course the new baby. In this book are Pietro's own reflections on the difficult years that followed, and how the example of his wife's serene and joyous faith helped sustain him through his grief at Gianna's death; when their little daughter, Mariolina, died only two years later; and through all the ordinary difficulties of raising a family alone—with the added extraordinary challenges of raising children whose absent mother had already become a revered public figure.

Almost immediately upon her death a devotion to Gianna arose among those whose lives she had so deeply touched, and who knew her heroic devotion to her faith and her family.

Her "cause" was introduced formally in 1970. She was

beatified April 24, 1994; and canonized on May 16, 2004 —forty-two years after her death.

That her husband, now ninety-one, and three children attended her canonization ceremony is one of several historic "firsts" connected with her canonization. (Pierluigi, an engineer, is married; Laura is a political scientist; Gianna Emanuela is a physician who specializes in Alzheimer's disease.)

Gianna Beretta Molla is the first married laywoman to be declared a saint (though there are many sainted widows). She is also the first canonized woman physician—a professional woman who was also a "working mom" four decades ago, when this was unusual.

Her witness of abiding faith in Christ, and her example of generous, loving self-donation—wherever and however she was called to serve the Lord—provide particular inspiration for women of our time and in our culture, where conflicting demands and confusing signals are a daily part of our lives.

There is another aspect of this new saint's life that is worth pondering—and this book affords a glimpse of it. That is, the role of her family—the example of her parents —in her formation as a committed, active young Catholic. Her family was outstanding for its deep Christian faith, expressed not only in worship, in private prayer and family devotions, but in generously extending their gift of faith to others.

Her family's example of unselfish love set the direction of young Gianna's life. It gave her the firm foundation upon which, through the grace of God and her trusting acceptance of his will for her, she confidently built her life—a life that would shelter, nurture, guide, and inspire countless others. Gianna's plans for raising her own children in the faith was influenced by her own experiences growing up. Her understanding of motherhood came from her own mother. Even though her own children could not know her tender motherly presence while they were growing up, she interceded for them. At the very end of her life, as Gianna suffered mortal pain, she sought her mother's prayers. As we—especially mothers of young families—may now seek hers.

Saint Gianna, pray for us.

> —Helen Hull Hitchcock
> Feast of Saint Joachim and Saint Anne
> July 26, 2004

PREFACE

"If you want to touch sanctity, go see Mr. Molla." That's the reply Father Renzo Cavallini gave me between calls on the cell phone he uses to take care of so many young people who look to him for answers and for a place where they can spend the night.

So I went to visit Mr. Molla, to approach the mystery of the life-giving encounter between a man and a woman, which the Church has once again proclaimed holy and blessed by God, the giver of life, by canonizing Gianna Beretta Molla.

The story of Doctor Beretta, who died in 1962 so her fourth child could live, has already been interpreted in several ways. At first, the emphasis was placed—perhaps excessively so—on her sacrifice, her brave decision to let the pregnancy come to term at the cost of her life. Then the focus shifted onto her whole life, from her years as a schoolgirl to those she spent as a university student, through her attainment of her specialization, when her fatiguing medical practice was accompanied by the exhausting work in the formation of the Young Women of Catholic Action.

Firmavit faciem suam (I have set my face like a flint [see Is 50:7c]), wrote Carlo Maria Cardinal Martini, the Archbishop of Milan, with his ability to find metaphors that define the meaning of a life. *Firmavit faciem suam* is a phrase that befits Gianna Beretta, who turned her deep gaze, her open, smiling face to God and kept them directed toward him in all occasions, in her everyday life, whether she bathed her children or chose the dress she would wear with her husband to La Scala. But that is not all. What is also of importance here is the mystery of the Incarnation and life of God, the Emmanuel, who draws close to mankind, the flesh that is the origin and the start of salvation. Here, the Church's teaching about the family becomes more credible (not by coincidence: Gianna Beretta was beatified during the Year of the Family), as a comparison is drawn between the family of Mary, Joseph, and Jesus and every family. For Gianna is not isolated in her sanctity, but rather her entire family feels the weight of God's glory and of his presence. With her family—her husband, Pietro, and her children, Pierluigi, Mariolina, Laura, and Gianna Emanuela—she bears witness that the flesh in which the Son of Man dwelt is the basis for salvation, a place where God is present. No one can take it as a scandal or abuse it out of lust or greed. To the puritans, today as yesterday, Jesus replies: "Will you also go away? . . . Truly, truly I say to you, unless you eat the flesh of the Son of man and drink his blood, you have no life in you" (Jn 6:67b, 53b). The flesh of a child, of a father, of a mother is like the flesh of the Son: it is a part of the mystery of salvation; it is sacred to God and to men.

Mr. Molla told me, "But I did not even realize I was living with a saint."

"True, but not even the apostles immediately understood that they were walking with the Son of God, [or] that the Immaculate One was in their midst—she who had never been touched by sin and concupiscence", I responded.

"But Gianna was a normal woman; she enjoyed life, she was happy, she loved her children."

"Mr. Molla, this is sanctity; this is the life God wanted to give mankind. But then the envious enemy sowed the evil seeds of hatred, envy, and resentment."

Gianna is a saint because she reminds us that life is beautiful, that God is happy when we climb a mountain to contemplate a snow-covered valley, when we help our brother, when we play with our children. Then there is the heavy load of pain and suffering. But we must not allow them to prevail. "Place your faith in God", says the psalmist. Gianna Beretta Molla was given to us to take the anxieties, fears, exhaustion, and suffering of every family and place them at God's feet, as a down payment on their joy and serenity.

The relationship between a saint and the Church of her time is shrouded in mystery: at times there is mutual acknowledgment, other times misunderstanding. Gianna was enthusiastically canonized by the Church. Our wish is that the Catholic community will become similar to the image of this woman—so joyful and outgoing, so affectionate and beautiful.

— Elio Guerriero

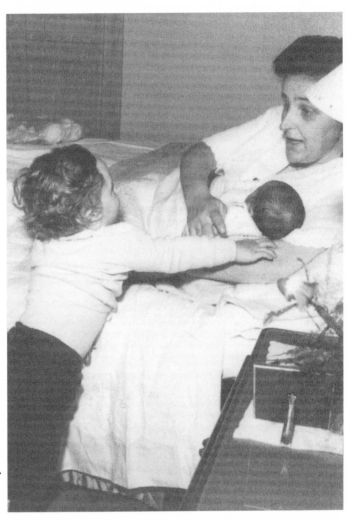

Saint Gianna with Pierluigi and
newborn Mariolina, December, 1957

INTRODUCTION

This book is comprised of three parts.

The first is a short presentation of the families of origin of Saint Gianna Beretta Molla, who was canonized on May 16, 2004. Here one finds the explanation of the dual last name, which is no aristocratic affectation, but rather bears witness to the nobility of a married woman, a mother, who had no wish to leave the upbringing of her children to the convent, but wanted to raise them up according to the teachings she and her husband had received from their respective families. Gianna was one of the Berettas of Piazza Risorgimento, strong Milanese folk that novelist Alessandro Manzoni would have liked. Pietro Molla came from Mesero, near Magenta, laborious and Christian in the best Lombard tradition.

The second part is an interview—at times more of a conversation—with Pietro Molla, the husband of this newly canonized woman. Saint Gianna seems to me to have a special flesh-and-blood quality, since her husband and her children are still among us, almost as if she were a precious sister offered as a gift to all families who daily need to live with joy and sorrow, exchanging goodbyes as they separate and greetings as they reunite, with long periods of work and short vacation breaks: in a word, life—the free gift we often feel as an unbearable burden in our day-to-day toiling. But Gianna's smile, her joy—never daunted by sorrow—invites us to have faith, and its foundation lies in Paul's words to the Philippians: "I thank my God in all my remembrance of you, always in every prayer of mine for you all making my prayer with joy" (Phil 1:3–4).

The third part is a reflection by Pietro Molla on Saint Gianna's virtues, in the form of a conversation with his wife: the Christian virtues of faith, hope, and charity; the human virtues of prudence, justice, fortitude, temperance, and perseverance. The reflection was prepared during the beatification process, and I believed it would be best to transcribe them in full, in all their beauty— stemming not so much from his literary skill, but from the deeply felt love that permeates them and gives them life.

Family and sanctity, therefore, are the themes of this work, whose main author is Mr. Pietro Molla, whom I thank from the bottom of my heart, not just for his generosity, but because he *lived* this book before he wrote it. In consenting to tell Gianna's story, he gives readers the precious treasure he found in his life: the sanctity of a wife bestowed by the Lord on the Molla family and on each and every family that still believes it possible to live the union between a man and a woman, and the upbringing of the children that may come, in a communion of love based on Christ. Mr. Molla thus honors the commitment he undertook when he consented to the beatification and canonization process: his Gianna, his bride, would be put forth as a model of Christian life, a life in the family, and hence would be in some ways taken away from his family for the good of all families. That is why I also wish to thank Saint Gianna's children and siblings, who shared this generosity. The Church has now officially recognized that, as Mr. Molla says, Gianna's example can do good. As Carlo Maria Cardinal Martini has written, Gianna has shown in the twentieth century (and continues to show us in the twenty-first century) "the meaning of a life lived as a vocation, a married life spent in joyous response to the Lord's calling".[1] For lay Christians, for families dealing with the myriad problems of daily life, Saint Gianna is a precious gift, a model to help us "cross the threshold of hope".

— Elio Guerriero

[1] Cardinal C. M. Martini, in John Paul II—Cardinal C. M. Martini, *Gianna Beretta Molla: A saint of the daily life* (Milan: Centro Ambrosiano [Ambrosian Center], 1994), p. 61.

Saint Gianna with Mariolina, Spring 1958

PART ONE

A Story of Three Generations

By Elio Guerriero

CHAPTER ONE

THE BERETTAS FROM MILAN

"A family like that", Cardinal Martini wrote,[1] in reference to Gianna Beretta's family, is a model for today's families. Her father, Alberto Beretta, was born into a large family at Magenta, September 23, 1889. Orphaned at the age of four, he became a boarder at the San Carlo diocesan school in Milan. His scholastic record was certainly good, but the boy deeply missed family warmth and closeness, so when he formed his own family, he always wanted to have his children near him. Gianna's mother, Maria De Micheli, was born on May 23, 1887. The first of five daughters, she completed trade school, which prepared her for a clerical job. However, Maria never had time to work in an office, for she was needed in the home. First she raised her sisters, then she married and had to think of her own family. As a young woman she had considered religious life, but her confessor helped her realize that the place destined for her was a family. She met Alberto, and the young couple, deeply in love and, filled with religious spirit, were married on October 12, 1908.

After the wedding the newlyweds established themselves in Piazza Risorgimento in Milan, not far from the Capuchin friary that became a reference point, a source

---

[1] Pamphlet published by the Centro Ambrosiano, Milan, 1994.

MAMMA MARIA, PAPA ALBERTO

Mamma was really the valiant woman of the Scriptures. Her day began early, at 5:00, when Papa awoke to go to early Mass and begin his day's work before the Lord and in the Lord's name. He went alone, because Mamma stayed home to prepare breakfast and, in a small lunch box, his midday meal.

When Papa left for work in Milan, Mamma passed through our bedrooms to awaken us, caressing our faces. We knew that shortly she would go to church to assist at Holy Mass, and we dressed quickly to go with her, happy to kneel beside her to prepare ourselves to receive Jesus in Holy Communion and to make our thanksgiving with her. What marvelous words she would suggest we tell Jesus! Then we would return home, have breakfast, and be off to school.

After Mamma straightened up the house and made our beds, she sat in her armchair beside a big basket overflowing with laundry to mend and socks to darn. She never complained, she always smiled, she never seemed tired. With all her work, she found time to meditate on a little book called *The Gift of Self*, written by a French author. One day, years later, I came across it, and reading it I seemed to see Mamma, who had so often reflected on those pages and translated them into her actions.

And Papa? He was a man of few words, but those few were the fruit of reflection and wisdom. His faith and piety were as great as Mamma's. He was a gentleman you could trust with your eyes closed. He came home each evening from Milan, and two or three of us would go to meet him at the railway station to carry his briefcase. Our chatter erased the signs of fatigue from his face, and it was enough for him to cross the threshold, to find Mamma's smile and the joyful reception of all his children, to completely recover his peace. It was supper time and everything was ready. After a short prayer we sat down happily at that long table. How beautiful it is for so many children to be around their parents!

He liked to hear a little from everyone about how school had gone, and when some peccadillo surfaced, he frowned to make us understand without saying anything that it should not happen again. After dinner, while Papa smoked his cigar, our older sister Amalia, an able pianist, played for us beautiful sonatas by Chopin, Bach, and Beethoven. Then came another important moment in the life of our family: the recitation of the Holy Rosary. Papa stood before the image of Our Lady with the older children while we younger ones were around Mamma, who helped us answer until we fell asleep leaning on her knees.

— *Testimony of Giuseppe Beretta*, in
Terra ambrosiana I (1994): 33–34

of spiritual support, and a place to find fellowship and to help their neighbor. Alberto was employed at the Cantoni cotton mill, where he was respected for his sense of responsibility and hard work. In those days there was no talk of family planning or "responsible parenthood". Parents welcomed children from the hand of God and trusted him for their upbringing and education. In this

spirit, Alberto and Maria had thirteen children. Three—
David, Rosina, and Pierina—died during the Spanish flu
epidemic; two others, Guglielmina and Anna Maria died
very young. In order of birth the other eight were: Amalia
(nicknamed Iucci), Francesco, Ferdinando, Enrico, Zita,
Giuseppe, Gianna, and Virginia. They frequently went
to the friary to play and see charity in action. Among
their friends were Maria and Luigi Gedda, who were to
become famous for their work in Catholic Action. But I
am getting ahead of myself.

To flee from the Spanish flu that had taken three of
his children, Alberto decided to move his family to Bergamo. He bought a pretty house with a garden in upper
Bergamo near their maternal grandparents' home and established the family there. For his part, every day Alberto
shuttled between Milan and Bergamo. It was an exhausting routine that began at 5:00 A.M. with Mass, and continued on the train, in the factory, and the train again to
return home. But when he came home, his fatigue and
worry gave way to joy in his family.

Gianna was born at her paternal grandparents' house
in Magenta (Milan) on the Feast of Saint Francis of As-
sisi, October 4, 1922, and she was consequently named
Giovanna Francesca. The move to Bergamo took place
three years later.

In a large family, some of the children have special tasks,
and special affinities are created, thanks to these. Other
bonds are formed because of closeness in age. Amalia, the
twenty-one-year-old eldest sister, prepared little Gianna
for her First Communion, which took place on April 14,
1928, in the parish of Santa Grata. Virginia, or Ginia, the

younger sister, was the one Gianna felt closest to. Gianna changed elementary school twice. The Canossian Sisters, with whom she studied during her last years of elementary school, had the most lasting influence on her. But during this period, school was not what mattered most to Gianna. She lived happily within her family. She accompanied her mother to Mass every day. Her mother and sister taught her to play the piano. She enjoyed life and nature. Upon finishing elementary school, she went on to the Paolo Sarpi School in Bergamo for the first four years of her secondary education. Her grades were not outstanding. In 1936 she failed Italian and Latin and was afraid of being kept back.

The next year was a turning point in the life of Gianna and of the Beretta family. Amalia, who had been sick for some time, died at the age of twenty-six. To allow his children to attend the university and to keep the family together, Alberto retired and moved the family to Genoa. Gianna continued high school with the Dorothean Sisters, where a gradual deepening in her religious education took place, a growth in faith that became apparent in 1938 when she made an Ignatian retreat directed by the Jesuit Father Avedano. Gianna was no longer the child who accompanied her mother to Mass, the junior member of Catholic Action, but a girl who wanted to take her destiny in her own hands and make her own choices before God: "I make the holy resolution to do everything for Jesus. All my works, all my disappointments, I offer everything to Jesus. . . . I want to ask the Lord to help me not go to hell. . . . I ask the Lord that he make me understand his great mercy." We might say that Gianna at this point was stepping out of her family upbringing to take her own path toward sanctity.

In the meantime, Gianna continued to play the piano and paint, but her health was not good. Her parents were concerned enough at the end of the school year (1938–1939) to decide to keep her at home. Thus, Gianna could be with her parents, to know them better, to study piano, and to devote her time to piety, which under the influence of the new pastor, the liturgist Monsignor Mario Righetti, acquired a markedly liturgical character. From then on, she habitually attended Mass, using the missal edited by Father Caronti, in order to follow better the readings and liturgical action.

In subsequent years, she returned to school, and the interruption and spiritual deepening had evidently served her well. She approached her studies with renewed vigor. She made plans for her life. She wanted to be a missionary and live the gospel. Following the example of her mother, whom Monsignor Righetti had encouraged to become president of the Catholic Action Women, Gianna began to lead the youngest Catholic Action girls. According to the pastor's testimony, she carried out her responsibilities with commitment and success. The Dorothean Sisters were also pleased with Gianna. Perhaps some already saw her as a future novice in their congregation.

It was an extraordinary time for the Beretta family: Francesco, left the oldest by Amalia's death, was about to become an engineer; Ferdinando, a physician; Zita, a pharmacist. Enrico and Giuseppe were at the university studying medicine and engineering, respectively, while Gianna and Virginia were finishing high school, in order to enter university life to study medicine. Clearly, the Beretta family exemplified Psalm 128:1, 3:

> Blessed is every one who fears the LORD, . . .
> Your wife will be like a fruitful vine
>   within your house;
> your children will be like olive shoots
>   around your table.

Initially, not even World War II disrupted this harmony, but the invidious enemy is always ready to lay traps and sow tares. Genoa was repeatedly bombed in 1941, and Maria Beretta, who already had heart trouble, was especially affected. The family hastily resolved to go home. It was summer, and for the time being they all went to their house at Viggiona on Lago Maggiore. It was the prelude to dispersion. In autumn the parents went back to Bergamo to live in the grandparents' home. Ferdinando had to enlist as a medical officer. Francesco and Zita began to work as an engineer and a pharmacist, respectively. Gianna and Virginia returned to Genoa to finish high school. Only Enrico and Giuseppe remained with their parents.

Alberto's health had been a source of concern for the family, but Maria was the first of the two to leave this world. Struck down by a cerebral thrombosis, she died on May 1, 1942, while Gianna, Ginia, and Enrico (who had hurried to Genoa to notify his sisters) traveled in anguish in a train that never seemed to arrive. Four months later, on September 1, the scene repeated itself, and Alberto was reunited with his Maria.

Enrico and Giuseppe decided to move again and went

to live at Magenta, where their paternal grandparents' house was available. Then during that same year, 1942, Giuseppe and Enrico left the family to become priests. Giuseppe entered the seminary at Bergamo. Enrico, already a physician, entered the Capuchin seminary at Lovere. Francesco, the engineer, became head of the family, while Gianna enrolled in medicine, first at Milan, then at Pavia, where Virginia joined her.

Gianna's days were structured by study and her commitments in Catholic Action. The happy, carefree girl from Bergamo had given way to a serious, hard-working young woman, devoted to medicine and to her Christian responsibility in Catholic Action for the formation of youth. But there was also room for joy—for trips to Viggiona and for mountain climbing. Her brothers provided other moments of happiness. Giuseppe was ordained a priest in the Bergamo Cathedral in 1946. Two years later it was Enrico's turn, as a Capuchin called Father Alberto, who departed for Brazil as a missionary. His example tugged at Gianna, who asked herself for a long time whether she ought not follow her brother. In 1949 Gianna graduated in medicine and surgery. The following year, Ferdinando was married, while Virginia finished medicine and took to the path of the missions.

In 1952 Gianna earned her specialization in pediatrics. Cardinal Martini has written: "I am impressed by the fact that Gianna and her siblings all achieved prestigious professional qualifications: two engineers, four physicians, a pharmacist, and a concert pianist. These results certainly reward the intellectual gifts and the conscientious effort of each of them. They also reflect the family's financial resources and prudent administration. But I believe that the determining factor was the parents' way of listening to their children."[3] The Beretta children felt understood and valued, and consequently they learned attention and respect for themselves and for others.

Gianna's life had arrived at a decisive stage. She seriously considered following Father Alberto to Brazil, but her health was not that required of a missionary. When he was consulted on the matter, Bishop Bernareggi of Bergamo responded bluntly: "In what my experience as priest and bishop has taught me, I know that when the Lord calls a soul to the missionary ideal, besides a great faith and an exceptional spirituality, he also gives physical strength that will help overcome difficulties and situations that here we are unable even to imagine. If Gianna does not have this gift, I think precisely that this is not the road the Lord calls her to live."[4]

With the removal of these doubts about her calling, the way of the family opened up to Gianna. Here she would find her true vocation to witness that the family is a place of grace and benediction. "In our own days too the Church is constantly enriched by the testimony of the many women who fulfill their vocation to holiness. Holy women are an incarnation of the feminine ideal; they are also a model for all Christians, a model of the *'sequela Christi'*, an example of how the Bride must respond with love to the love of the Bridegroom" (*Mulieris dignitatem*, no. 27). This was the life that was opening up before Gianna.

---

[3] *Una famiglia così*, p. 23.
[4] Testimony given by her brother Father Giuseppe Beretta, in *Terra ambrosiana* 1 (1994): 36.

Saint Gianna feeds Mariolina at a picnic,
with Pierluigi looking on

CHAPTER TWO

THE MOLLAS FROM MESERO

Like an account of two tributaries that converge into one mighty river, we must take a quick look at the other branch of the family before describing the shared life of Gianna Beretta and Pietro Molla.

Pietro Molla, as we will soon see, was to become Gianna Beretta's husband. His father, Luigi, was born in 1884 at Mesero, a little town between Magenta and Busto Arsizio. An apprentice shoemaker at eight, he became the manager of the Mesero branch of a Parabiago shoe factory at twenty-one and is still remembered in the town as the person who taught all of the shoemakers in the region. In 1907 he married Maria Salmoiraghi, who worked in a silk factory. Eight children were born to the couple, but the first three died very young. The first to survive past infancy was Pietro, born at Mesero on July 1, 1912, followed by Rosetta, Adelaide, Luigia, and Teresina. Luigi's hopes were deposited in his son. He dreamed that the boy might become an engineer and encouraged him to study at the cost of considerable sacrifice.

The first difficulty was that only the initial grades of elementary school existed in Mesero, and to continue his education it was necessary for Pietro to pass the fifth-year examination. With the help of the pastor, Luigi turned to the dear Sisters recently established in the town. Their superior, Mother Giovanna Calloni, gave the boy his fifth-grade lessons and taught him dedication and generosity at the same time. He passed the fifth-grade examination as Fascism was consolidating its dictatorship. Luigi was forced to find a boarding school for his son so that he could attend the five years of middle school. He selected the Villoresi San Giuseppe School at Monza, then run by the Barnabite Fathers. The atmosphere was strict, but Pietro gladly committed himself to study to please his father, who had placed such trust in him. However, it seems he suffered from the premature separation from his family. In San Giuseppe he found good priests who taught him Latin and respect for others, but the discipline was rigid, and the pedagogy's excessive emphasis on obligation to study and work was inappropriate for younger boys. Pietro met these difficulties, providing a source of pride for his father. (Luigi was himself a person of great rectitude, to whom the pastor entrusted the administration of the Catholic mutual aid society and whom the town made its justice of the peace.) After finishing middle school in 1928, Pietro remained at Villoresi San Giuseppe School as a prefect, a person responsible for the discipline of a group of younger boys, and enrolled at the Bartolomeo Zucchi Public High School in Monza. It is not difficult to see in these decisions the young man's desire not to burden the family finances excessively.

After his final examinations in 1931, Pietro finally went home. Luigi was proud of the son who had brought honor along with his grades, and he was not apprehensive when Pietro chose to attend the polytechnical institute to become an engineer. Sacrifices would be necessary at home, but the son could continue to study. The trip—by bicycle from Mesero to Magenta and by train from Magenta to Milan—was a trifle for Pietro, but he faced demands on his time from several sides. There was a Party head who wanted to put him in charge of the local Fascist group. The pastor wanted him in Catholic Action. Appreciative of the trust placed in him, Pietro accepted both positions. He devised a system of distributing government food assistance for families, based on an accurate analysis of needs. He organized the promulgation of birth and marriage certificates, as well as the assistance for children to attend summer camp. For the parish priest he was present Sunday afternoons in church for adult catechesis.

Despite all these commitments, which often left him overworked, he obtained his degree in mechanical engineering from the Milan Polytechnical Institute in 1936. Graduates had no problems finding work in that time. He had contact with the Tosi Company but before the end of 1936 went to work in the Saffa Company's large match factory located at Ponte Nuovo di Magenta, a few kilometers from home. He was associate manager by 1938, with much older people who had spent their lives at Saffa under his supervision. The young executive was notable for great devotion to work and for attention to the diversification of labor and new technology. "By comparison to Gianna, I have done very little in the strictly ecclesiastical field. I have worked a great deal, certainly. I have tried all my life to create jobs. This has been my life." Meanwhile, however, his membership in Catholic Action saved him from subsequent involvement with Fascism. For many years the disputes between Pius XI and

Mussolini on account of Catholic Action Youth had few repercussions at Mesero. Once war broke out, everything became more rigid. In December 1940, Pietro received three communications: he was informed of the cancellation of his posts in the Party and in the National Balilla Activity, and he was obliged to return his university militia uniform: "All because I was enrolled in Catholic Action. How can I not see it as a sign of Providence?"

After a moment of confusion, our Saffa executive immersed himself even more deeply in his work of trying to develop his factory to the utmost and putting in practice the respect for others, which he esteems as the most precious inheritance from his father, a support that saved his life several times. In March 1944 he was arrested for the first time with three workers: the Communist Pietro Gerassi and the Socialists Armando Armi and Giuseppe Martini. Transferred to Magenta, they were about to be loaded onto a bus that was to hand them over to the Germans. Alerted by a Saffa workman, Umberto Parmigiani, head of the local Fascist Party, arrived. After long negotiations he succeeded in obtaining the release of young Molla, whom he knew for his work at Mesero, and the other three detainees as well. About a year later, just days before Mussolini's execution, Pietro was arrested again. This time engineer Molla and the factory director, Francesco Bordone, were already on the bus destined to the concentration camp when Parmigiani arrived again. Again there were exhausting negotiations ending in release.

But the war had not ended. Two days after the liberation of Milan, near the Saffa factory there was still a

German antiaircraft battery at the bridge over the Ticino River. The soldiers were all the more nervous as defeat and surrender came closer. An American tank column arrived from Milan, headed to Novara, and was eager for action. There were employees, civilians, and the plant to protect. This time engineer Molla conducted the negotiations. Thanks to the providential presence of a colleague, Giuseppe Megler, who spoke German and English well, he invited the heads of the two opposing detachments to his office and sent his driver to Como so the German officer could seek authorization to surrender from his commander, General Wolf.

With patience and good sense the negotiation succeeded: the Germans surrendered with no bloodshed. The factory was saved and could resume its activity shortly. It was certainly a minor episode in the general development of the war, but thanks to the cool nerves of the associate manager, the Saffa quickly reached full production during reconstruction.

The engineer was not satisfied with equaling what had been previously accomplished and, realizing that his company should not limit itself to matches, sought other fields of work. He traveled in Italy and abroad, visiting Swedish and American factories in particular. The boy who had lived *The Tree of the Wooden Shoes* ("In winter they went to the stable to get warm") now crossed Europe and the world to look for areas of production with advanced technology. In 1950 he was named central director of the company's factories. His incessant activity left him no time for feelings or other diversions, but the year of the promotion brought a humanizing sorrow. His twenty-seven-year-old sister, Teresina, the baby of the family, fell seriously ill and died. As a child she had been stricken by nephritis, which had not been properly diagnosed and treated. Thus, the illness returned with a vengeance and conquered the young woman, despite the efforts of a physician named Beretta. In these circumstances Pietro and Doctor Beretta did not even exchange a word. Their next meeting would be different. Then their lives would be joined in the sacrament that bears witness to the spousal love of Christ and the Church and engenders new life, drawing on the fecundity of the Father, who of his love gives life to every person and every creature.

CHAPTER THREE

THE BERETTA-MOLLAS

How Gianna and Pietro became engaged and then married is quickly told. After a few casual encounters, the couple met at the end of 1954 at the celebration after the first Mass of Father Lino Garavaglia, now Bishop of Cesena. A friendship was born based on mutual respect and shared ideals (work, family, love of neighbor) regarding their intentions for a family open to God, to children, to sacrifices, and to suffering.

Gianna was a beautiful woman with a penetrating look, and Pietro soon fell in love. She drew him out of the solitude and monotony of the factory routine. On his side, Pietro gave security to the young woman, who had lost her parents and had been seeking her road for some time. From two paths one began to emerge, one that would give room for life and joy, for hikes in the mountains, concerts at the Scala, and Sunday gatherings.

Gianna envisaged a Christian family as a cenacle gathered around Jesus. For the first time Pietro, who had grown up in an atmosphere that smacked of Jansenism, felt free from the burdens of responsibility and could laugh and joke. The dates of the engagement and wedding, April 11 and September 24, 1955, respectively, were set, announcing to relatives and friends Gianna and Pietro's

I FEEL SO HAPPY IN
TOUCH WITH NATURE

Dearest Pietro,

Today at noon at my return from the ski trip, I found your special delivery letter. You can imagine how much it delighted me with your sweet affectionate expressions, which show all the love you have for me. Thank you, dear Pietro. I love you too and so much, and I think that we will love each other always. You have such a good disposition, and you are so intelligent that you always make me understand, so we can't help but agree. I'm sorry that you had so much work Monday. I always follow you with my thought, and if I could help, I would do it with all my heart.

Yesterday and today we had splendid sunshine. I get up in the morning at eight (what a loafer! You are already at the factory!) because Mass is at eight-thirty. Believe me, I have never enjoyed Holy Mass and Communion as much as in these days. The chapel, so beautiful and recollected, is empty. The celebrant has not even an altar boy, so the Lord is all for me and for you, Pietro, because now where I am, you are too.

We leave immediately after breakfast with our skis. Around eleven I go to the ski teacher and have a little class, and modesty apart, I have learned to make even difficult descents. But don't worry, there is no danger, because where the slope is too steep, the teacher makes us go down by an easier path. But it is marvelous.

When you are up high, with a clear sky, pure white snow, how you enjoy yourself and praise God!

Pietro, you already know it; I feel so happy when I am in touch with nature, which is so beautiful that I would spend hours contemplating it.

After lunch, after a short rest and walk, we come back to the camp about three and stay there until about six. Then time would go slowly. Fortunately I have the dear company of Piera, a lovely, happy sort, and we laugh so much!

There is my day, a little different from yours; poor Pietro, always working.

Two more days now and then we will see each other —what a joy!

Goodbye, dear Pietro; give my best regards to your parents and your sister Adelaide, and have a big hug from your affectionate

Gianna

Piera thanks you and returns your greeting.

— Letter of March 23, 1955,
from Gianna to Pietro Molla

faith in a decision taken in their hearts: to make the vow of love that knows no limits. Gianna and Pietro were real people, two young people in love who lived their engagement with joy and waited impatiently for their wedding day. Gianna, in particular, was happy and not afraid to express her feelings. She chose the furniture for their house, bought towels and linens, thought about her wedding dress. Then on September 24 Gianna and Pietro met before the altar.

It is worth dwelling on this moment: "Dressed in white satin with a veil of tulle, tied at her neck, she enters the basilica of Saint Martin at Magenta on the arm of her brother Ferdinando. Her Pietro, full of emotion, waits at the altar."[1] Gianna is beautiful because she is the image of woman and the Church, the image of the bride, whose love "many waters cannot quench . . . neither can floods drown it" (Song 8:7). Those present perceive this beauty, which shines like a great light, and show their admiration with applause, which breaks out in the silence of the church: "My beloved is mine and I am his, he pastures his flock among the lilies" (Song 2:16). Gianna and Pietro were to demonstrate soon that the commitment of love made that day before Father Giuseppe, their priest-brother, was stronger than any difficulty, even than death.

The festivities were genuine and were followed by a honeymoon trip in southern Italy: Rome, Naples, Ischia, and Taormini were the primary stops. Daily life together began upon their return, but Gianna and Pietro did not complain about life's hardships—the seemingly endless duration of the work week, with rest and holidays fleetingly short. Gianna particularly was a "calm woman, full of joy. A joy which particularly irradiated and seemed to infect all those around her".[2] She was involved more than ever as a general practitioner and pediatrician, but

---

[1] G. Pelucchi, *Gianna Beretta Molla* (Milan: San Paolo, 1994).

[2] Testimony of Father Agostino Cerri, reported in ibid., p. 74.

she did not forget the Catholic Action Women, nor did she neglect the big Beretta family; she wrote faithfully to her siblings who were far away and visited those who lived close by. Nando, the physician-brother whose office she had shared for a time, had a little girl (called Iucci in memory of their sister Amalia), the favorite of Aunt Gianna, who took her home as often as she could.

Doctor Beretta seemed to have a natural inclination for motherhood, and it was not long before she was with child. She confided the news to her husband with delicacy but with great joy. November 19, 1956, their first child, Pierluigi, was born. With him began a custom that would be faithfully reenacted at subsequent births: he was baptized and consecrated to Our Lady of Good Counsel. December 11 the following year saw the birth of Maria Zita, nicknamed Mariolina. Two years later came Laura on July 15, 1959. Gianna did not have easy pregnancies or births, but she willingly faced the sacrifices of motherhood: "When a woman is in travail she has sorrow, because her hour has come; but when she is delivered of the child, she no longer remembers the anguish, for joy that a child is born into the world" (Jn 16:21). So it was for Gianna, who was radiant after every delivery, sure of having taken part in God's creative action. God created heaven, earth, the sun, the sea, and man, and "saw that it was good". Gianna saw in her children the goodness of God and the guarantee that the world was destined not only to stagnation and decay, but also to renewal and new life and the continual transmission of generations.

"The heavens are telling the glory of God; and the firmament proclaims his handiwork", says Psalm 19:1.

SISTERS ARE PRECIOUS

Dearest Mariuccia,

I don't know whether you already received the announcement. Wednesday morning at 8:15 Lauretta was born. You cannot imagine our joy, first of all because, thank God, everything went well. Then, because she is beautiful, good, healthy, and then, because she is a girl, and I really wanted a little sister for Mariolina. I know by experience how precious sisters are, and so the Lord heard my prayers.

A month ago, the fifteenth to be exact, I had to go to the emergency room to be treated for poisoning. I had very strong pains, continuous spasmodic contractions, fever, and vomiting—I ran the risk of losing my child. Terrified, I obeyed Nando and let myself be taken to Monza. It was already midnight and the professor of obstetrics, who knew me well, was already waiting for me. So with oxygen, tranquilizers, and hypodermoclisis everything went away, and two days later I could go to the Malpensa Airport to meet Pietro, who was returning from America without knowing anything. I hoped to come back with the newborn . . . and instead I continued my pregnancy undaunted to the end, with my usual ten days delay, and now here I am with my Lauretta, such a good baby. In these three days of life, she sleeps, nurses a little, and almost never cries. I'm sorry I can't show her to you, but her hair is dark, really black (she has more than Mariolina at a year and a half!), light-colored eyes, and she weighed eight pounds, eleven ounces at birth. Her face is somewhat oval-shaped; she looks more like Gigetto than my little girl. This evening I am expecting my two treasures, who have been at Courmayeur for two weeks now. Every day they phone me because this year I could have a telephone in the cottage, and they are delighted to come to see the "new little sister" (because Pierluigi calls her that). Yesterday evening he wanted me to put her on the phone: "I want to talk with my little sister."

I am curious to see his expression this evening and what he will do near the cradle. He has already said that he "won't whack the new kid, but the old kid, yes".

Excuse me, Mariucciona, my long chattering, but it does not seem real this time not to have you near me now.

Give my warm regards to Aunt Ninì and a big kiss to your Pierangelo, whom I imagine handsome, lively, and full of health.

Cordial greetings to Giampiero, and to you a big hug from your most affectionate

Gianna

Lots of greetings to everyone from Zita, who, as always, is here and attends me with so much concern and affection.

— *Letter from Gianna to Mariuccia Parmigiani, dated July 18, 1959*

Thus Gianna was happy whenever she could take the children to Courmayeur in the mountains of the Acosta Valley. There the air is good, and there she could ski and walk and participate in the praising of God, which day and night on peaks and in valleys proclaims his grace and mercy, beauty and providence. Just as God, after having created man, sustains him at every moment, so parents are called to a gift without end, to transmit the breath of life to children.

In *Mulieris dignitatem*, Pope John Paul II offers his interpretation of the words of Jesus in regard to the suffering and joy of childbirth: "The first part of Christ's words refers to the 'pangs of childbirth' which belong to the heritage of original sin; at the same time these words indicate *the link that exists between the woman's motherhood and the Paschal Mystery*" (no. 19). The passion, death, and resurrection of Jesus is what every woman experiences to some degree in childbirth, but Gianna seemed called to a higher degree of participation. She was invited, as Saint Paul says, to descend into the grave with Christ to confer new life, to witness that from death life is born, that the most dreadful and real suffering is not the last word, that it has not won the battle, but must yield to the new light of Easter, to life in God.

After Laura's birth in 1959 Gianna wrote to her friend Mariuccia of her joy at having given a playmate to Mariolina. Perhaps she wanted to give a brother to Pierluigi as well, perhaps she desired a big family like her husband's and her own. In fact, in the second half of 1961 she announced a new pregnancy. Initially, the symptoms were like those of previous pregnancies, but soon the situation became more serious because of a fibroid tumor that threatened the life of mother and child. Normal medical practice then current could have eliminated any risk for the mother by removing the diseased uterus, but Gianna was opposed to sacrificing the baby's life for her own.

She understood the risk she was taking, but her vocation as physician and mother was to support life, not to threaten it. "Although she was a physician", many have written, she put the life of her child in the first place. "Precisely because she was a physician", I would correct them, she felt reinforced in her choice as mother and ordered her husband and attending physician to place the baby's life before hers. But at this point the die was not yet cast. At the beginning of September she had a seemingly successful operation and the pregnancy continued its course.

Certainly, in the back of Gianna's and Pietro's minds was a dark foreboding that periodically emerged to the surface of their consciousness. But both spouses were convinced that Gianna would live. Gianna loved life; she wanted to accompany her husband and raise her precious children. Pietro trusted in Providence; he believed that God would not abandon a family that offered him so many supplications and who trusted him completely. Did not the Lord say one day that when two were gathered in his name he would be with them and the Father would hear them? (see Mt 18:19). But with God, nothing can be taken for granted. His ways are not our ways. Gianna entered the hospital on April 20, 1962; the following morning her fourth child was born. Again, it was a girl in perfect health, and they named her Gianna Emanuela. The mother's condition, however, worsened progressively. She was diagnosed as having septic peritonitis, which gradually overcame her resistance. After great suffering, she died on

April 28, 1962. She was thirty-nine years old. What fool-
ishness! But it is a madness of the same quality as that of
Jesus: "Do you not know that all of us who have been baptized into Christ Jesus were baptized into his death? We
were buried therefore with him by baptism into death,
so that as Christ was raised from the dead by the glory of
the Father, we too might walk in newness of life" (Rom
6:3–4).

And Pietro? I wonder if he had read a draft of a poem
that a nineteenth-century Lombardic writer, who sang
well of trust in Providence, wrote at the death of his
wife after having prayed in vain for her cure. Alessandro
Manzoni wrote:

> Yes, you are terrible
> . . .
> You see our tears,
> You hear our cries,
> You question our will,
> And at your will decide.

The author of the *The Betrothed* never published that
poem, recognizing its blasphemy. God is not deaf to our
prayer, nor is he incapable of pity and affection, as it seems
in our darker hours. His suffering and death were greater
than that of any man, and our suffering and death are near
to him, are manifestations of his love. Is it any wonder,
then, that those whom God holds dearest are chosen to
testify to his unsurpassing love through the manner of
their death? "O the depth of the riches and wisdom and
knowledge of God! How unsearchable are his judgments
and how inscrutable his ways!" (Rom 11:33).

Gianna Beretta Molla is associated with the paschal mystery of Christ, to witness to his love and his presence among men. The beauty of Gianna is a glimpse of the beauty of God and the drama of his love.

PART TWO

Saint Gianna, My Wife
An Interview with Pietro Molla

By Elio Guerriero

Gianna Beretta and Pietro Molla during their engagement

CHAPTER ONE

ENGAGEMENT AND MARRIAGE

How did you meet your wife?

I saw Gianna for the first time in 1950,[1] when I went to the Magenta Hospital to visit my twenty-seven-year-old sister, Teresina. She had nephritis, which had been incorrectly diagnosed and treated as a child, and was near the end. By then none of the doctors' remedies helped, and Teresina died a week later. So, I saw the woman doctor who was giving my sister a transfusion, but we did not exchange a word. A year later, I visited Gianna's brother, who was also a physician at Magenta. He had a practice, and I needed help with a sore throat. There, I saw Gianna again, but once more we did not talk.

In 1950–1951 Gianna opened an office at Mesero across the street from my parents' house. I lived at Monte Nuovo di Magenta, and when I went to Mesero we would cross paths. I knew she was a wonderful girl, that she was also well known at Mesero for her talks to young women in Catholic Action. We actually became acquainted on the Feast of the Immaculate Conception in 1954. A Capuchin Father, Lino Garavaglia, now Bishop of Cesena

[1] Later Pietro Molla recalls an earlier encounter in September 1949. See below, p. 117.

and Sarsina, celebrated his First Mass on that occasion. I
was invited as a fellow townsman, Gianna as family doctor and friend. We met there. I was attracted to her. First
I saw her kneeling in church, then at dinner we wound up
opposite each other. In fact I wrote in my diary: "Thanking God, I think I made a good acquaintance."

From then on, I managed to find opportunities for us
to meet. The first time was at a ballet in Milan on New
Year's Eve, 1954.

How did acquaintance turn into love?

Talking with Gianna, my good first impression was confirmed quickly. I found her an extraordinarily transpar-
ent person, extraordinarily gracious. Her looks, her attitude, her eyes, her beauty made her very attractive. I
understood that she was right for me, that I would like
to be with her. So, I had fallen in love, but I did not find
words to express my feelings. Thank God, Gianna was
more effusive, more open. By contrast, my temperament
was more reserved because of my upbringing and life experiences.

As a boy, I studied at the San Giuseppe School in
Monza, where I was the prefect during my secondary
school years, that is, I was responsible for the younger
boys. Later, as soon as I completed my engineering studies, I went to work at Saffa, a factory with four thousand
employees. A year and a half later, I was named associate
manager. Therefore, my life has been marked, so to speak,
by responsibility.

Returning to 1954, I found a complement in this

woman, who was more open, more effusive than myself. Confirmation came at the beginning of 1955. After our meeting at the ballet we met a couple of times at her house in January. Then at the beginning of February she wrote me a letter: "I must tell you right away that I am a woman who wants affection very much; I have found you, and I intend to give myself totally in order to form a *truly* Christian family." In subsequent letters, her joy, her faith, her humanity, her thanking the Lord for all the good things he gives, came across clearly.

Still, before knowing you, Gianna had the intention of following her brother to Brazil.

I knew this after we were married, which was providential. With my temperament, if I had known it before, I would never have been capable of approaching a young lady who had that kind of intention. Besides, thinking back now to the way in which Gianna lived her vocation to marriage, to the way in which she behaved with me from the very first day of our engagement, I could never have thought that she had any inclination toward a vocation to a religious order or anything close. Indeed, she embraced the vocation to marriage enthusiastically, full of joy.

On the other hand, the desire to go to Brazil seems logical. Having a brother who was a missionary doctor at Grajaù (in the southern Amazon region) and who needed help badly, she intended to follow him. She did not because of different obstacles, and when, through the advice of her confessor, she understood that her vocation was marriage, she embraced it quite deliberately.

What were the stages of your relationship?

Being certain that she was a wonderful girl and that we loved each other, we decided to proceed fairly quickly toward marriage. Neither of us, in fact, was very young anymore. So, we met at the end of 1954, and we were engaged in April 1955. At that time, she suggested: "Pietro, let's begin our official engagement with Holy Mass and Communion in the Canossian Sisters' chapel."

It was a marvelous time. Gianna and I were exuberant. There are pictures that, so to speak, catch the fullness of Gianna's joy. For example, there is a photo taken in the summer of 1955, on the snows of Livrio at Bormio. Our joy was deeply felt, clear, real. Then, three weeks before the wedding, set for September 24, she wrote me a letter: "There are three weeks left. Then I will be Gianna Molla. What would you say if we prepared for marriage with a triduum?" I was very glad to make it with her, but it would never have come into my head to prepare ourselves that way. Ten days before the wedding she wrote me again: "I would like our new family to be a cenacle gathered around Jesus."

You often speak of letters from your wife. Can you tell us something more?

Certainly, some of the most touching "relics" that I keep of my wife are precisely the letters from our engagement. I have others from when we were married, but they often talk about the children and about married life. However, the letters in which Gianna expressed her ideas on marriage, the vision she had of preparation for marriage,

GRATITUDE FOR THE RING

My dearest Pietro,

How can I thank you for the magnificent ring? Dear Pietro, to reciprocate, I give you my heart, and I will always love you as I love you now.

I think that when we were about to get engaged, you were pleased to know that you are the one dearest to me, the one to whom my thoughts, affections, and desires return continually. I only wait for the moment in which I can be yours forever.

Pietro dearest, you know that it is my wish to see and know you are happy. Tell me how I should be and what I should do to make you happy.

I have so much trust in the Lord, and I am certain that he will help me be a worthy spouse to you.

I like to meditate often on the first reading for the Mass of Saint Anne: "Who shall find a valiant woman? . . . The heart of her husband trusteth in her. . . . She will render him good, and not evil, all the days of her life." (Prov 31:10–12)

Pietro, I wish I could be the valiant woman of the Scripture for you! Instead, I feel weak. I feel so safe near you! I ask you a favor from today on, Pietro. If you see that I do something that is not right, tell me, correct me. Do you understand? I will always be thankful.

With so very much affection, I embrace you, and I wish you a holy Easter.

Your Gianna

— Letter from Gianna to Pietro, April 9, 1955

the way in which she prepared herself for the sacrament of love, and the joy she experienced in anticipation of this event are those from our engagement. But there is more. In those letters there is also her joy in the beauty and charm of creation to which, on her side, she corresponded with an attitude of gratefulness and thanks to the Creator. She also encouraged me to share those feelings. She wrote: "Pietro, I wish I could be the valiant woman of the Scripture for you! Instead, I feel weak. . . . I have so much trust in the Lord, and I am sure that he will help me be a spouse worthy of you."

Trust in the Lord and the invitation to prayer were the recurring themes of her letters.

One gets the impression that your wife gave you an education of sorts.

Certainly, a complete education, even from the human point of view. Because at the very moment when she invited me to participate in the liturgy or in acts of piety, she proposed a new model of humanity to me. As soon as we were engaged, I had to confess to her that I worked too much: every day until late, including Saturdays, and many times Sunday, too. She said to me right away: "That's not right; it's good to work, but you also have to rest and have fun. Look how beautiful concerts are; let's subscribe to concerts. Plays are delightful too." So we bought season tickets for concerts and plays. She taught me to live better.

Therefore, engagement was, as it always ought to be, a beautiful and joyous period.

I still should underline that Gianna's effusiveness was decisive for me, her taking the initiative unexpectedly to send me beautiful letters. Now they are so much more welcome because words can be forgotten while writings are still here and can be read and meditated over. Also, there is her spontaneous generosity. From the beginning and in almost all the letters she comes back to this request: "Tell me what I should do to make you happy." It wasn't difficult for me to correspond to this love of hers. If she wanted to make me happy, what could my purpose be if not to make her happy? In this way, too, she helped me to be less introverted, to throw away the mask in dealings with other people.

Probably the large number of her friends and acquaintances came from that spontaneity.

I think so. Gianna had a wealth of character. She was a strong, decisive person.

With marriage came children. How did you prepare for the birth of the first child? How did you receive him?

Gianna and I desired to have more than one child. We loved life and wanted others to have it. As she wrote me during our engagement, she considered the birth of children a grace the Lord grants to married people. Gianna was a joyful person, but when a child was born, her joy was full and perfect. Nothing was lacking. She was radiant. From the beginning of our marriage she prepared herself with prayer to create the most welcoming, the most serene environment for our children.

Then there was the consecration to Our Lady. We lived in Ponte Nuovo, and two minutes away from our house there was a chapel dedicated to Our Lady of Good Counsel. At the end of each child's baptism, at Gianna's request, I read the act of consecration to Our Lady of Good Counsel. Gianna was very devoted to her, and I think that her final choices were brought to maturity in the shadow of the Madonna of Good Counsel.

We also prepared for the arrival of children with some trepidation, asking ourselves, like everyone, whether we would be able to raise them well. Later, we had another little cross. After the birth of the first child, we asked ourselves: "If we have other children, how will we manage to love them like this one?" We were so much in love with the first one that it seemed impossible to us to love other children with the same intensity. But, as parents know well, love is something spontaneous.

Another of Gianna's traits was the great importance she gave to the children's birth. The arrival of the children was the grace par excellence. Therefore, although she was a doctor, she would say to me that it is good for children to be born at home within the family. So it was for the first three children. The doctor and nurse were there, but the birth occurred at home.

Then the family was a community, a communion of life and love.

Yes, an open community. We had a welcoming home. Especially at holidays, Gianna invited all our close relatives to our house. There were twenty of us—a big, lovely family. This openness came to Gianna from her family.

We can say your life was beautiful. However, it rested on prayer.

Certainly. We said the Rosary every day. Besides, Gianna went to Mass every morning, and when she was unable to do so, she never failed to go to the chapel of Our Lady of Good Counsel for a moment of prayer and meditation. She also taught our children to pray. Unfortunately, she died when they were still little, but she set them on the way to prayer early on.

Did you pray together?

Yes, in the evening, before going to bed.

Saint Gianna with Mariolina in San Vigilio, Bergamo, 1958

CHAPTER TWO

CATHOLIC LAITY

Your wife was deeply involved in the life of the Church. You have worked in Catholic volunteer organizations yourself. Probably your family upbringing led you to this choice. Can you talk to us about it?

Obviously, in what concerns my wife, I can respond only on the basis of reports from others and of Gianna's writings. From the latter it is apparent that, like me, she received an upbringing that encouraged us to accept the gift of faith wholeheartedly, to see Jesus himself in one's neighbor, and to involve oneself as much as possible in spreading the gospel, so that others too might have the gift of faith, joy, and the grace of God. Moreover, in the Franciscan spirit she received from the Capuchin Fathers on Viale Piave, Gianna had special concern for the poor. Later, she nourished the upbringing she received from her parents with prayer, retreats, and membership in Catholic Action. Here, she made the gifts she received from her family flourish. It was not difficult for me to attune myself to Gianna's disposition, because I also had the gift of a very good family. I too had the gift of wonderful parents and a wonderful priest. If I had to sum up the essence of my formation as a Catholic layman in one single concept, I would choose respect for my neighbor. Both parents and priests of Catholic Action taught me great respect for others, and this attitude has been invaluable for me in my life. In the decades I spent in factories with positions of great responsibility, precisely respect for my neighbor saved me in the Fascist years, during the war, and in the period of great strikes.

From the family to the Church. Was Gianna's upbringing at home complemented by the formation she received from the clergy and religious who influenced her?

From what she told me herself, Monsignor Righetti, her confessor, had a decisive influence in Gianna's development. When Gianna passed away, he wrote me a touching letter. Monsignor Righetti, a famous liturgist, carried out his ministry at Genoa Quinto, where Gianna's family moved in 1938 after the great sadness of her sister Amalia's death. Her father decided to move the family to the capital of Liguria to let his children breathe better air and to attend university more easily. There, Gianna finished middle school and attended the high school run by the Dorothean Sisters, and in 1938, at the age of sixteen, she made a retreat with a Jesuit, Father Avedano, which turned out to be decisive. In the three days of retreat, she received so many graces that her life underwent a major change. In particular, she deepened her devotion for Jesus and for the Virgin Mary.

So, Gianna had an excellent Christian education, but then in turn she was an educator, in particular of Catholic Action Youth.

Yes, her family and she were always close to Catholic Action, which Gianna joined at the age of twelve. Meanwhile, at Monsignor Righetti's insistence, her mother was elected president of Catholic Action Women at Genoa Quinto. Right after the war, Gianna was in charge of the youngest girls in Catholic Action and later became president of the Young Women. Perhaps it is worth recalling the testimony her girls give about her. Even today, Gianna is for them the delegate and the earnest, approachable president, who invited them to joy and to Christian life. Reading the notes for her conferences to the young women, you get an idea of the commitment with which Gianna fulfilled her responsibility, of the profound spirituality that she absorbed and tried to transmit. She encouraged each girl to be in the grace of God and to become a saint, but also to act in her own particular way. She often repeated: "Christian life is not achieved by people who do little but by those who commit themselves completely."

WE WILL BRING JOY EVERYWHERE: THE FRAGRANCE OF CHRIST

When the soul is in the grace of God, it becomes one with God—a temple of God. "If a man loves me, he will keep my word, and my Father will love him, and we will come to him, and make our abode in him" [Jn 14:23].

Not a temporary abode but a permanent one, and Christ remains unless we drive him out by sin.

When we make our Communion, as long as the Species last, we are physically joined to Jesus Christ so that we may say with Saint Paul: "It is not I who live, but Christ who lives in me" [Gal 2:20b].

When the Species cease to be there, Jesus disappears physically but remains in us mystically all day. Thus, our hearts are the living cenacles, the monstrances through whose glass the world ought to see Christ.

Girls, if we were truly convinced of this, how much better would we behave all day long.

The thought that ought to stay with us this week is: To be an apostle, that is, to belong to Catholic Action, the soul ought always to be in grace, that is, ought to be the temple, the living tabernacle; I ought to have the divine life in me to be able to communicate it to the souls that surround me. Let us often think that with grace, with Jesus in our hearts, we are "Alter Christus". We will certainly not only keep from committing sin, but we will bring joy everywhere, the fragrance of Christ.

— *Conference to the Young Women of*
Catholic Action, October 28, 1946

Excuse an observation: I have the impression that your wife received a careful but also rather conventional religious formation. At some point, however, a kind of shift occurred, a new emphasis that came not so much from theoretical teaching as from her nature, from her sensibility, and it constitutes the specific character of her sanctity.

I agree and confirm your impression with an example. Once retreats were made in special houses, directed by religious or priests, where the day was spent in meditation and silence. However, Gianna brought her young women to Viggiona, to the family's country house, where they did meditate and pray, but at the same time alternated these religious practices with walks and picnics, with songs. So the retreats acquired new joy and serenity. I feel able to say that Gianna was ahead of the times and was a pioneer in her capacity to know how to live her faith with joy. It may be that her joy and love of nature came also from her closeness to Franciscan spirituality.

There is another important aspect. Today we speak of volunteer organizations. Reading about your wife, I have the impression that she had an extraordinary understanding of the role of volunteers, intuiting needs, anticipating requests, getting involved without sparing herself, with great attentiveness and eagerness.

Gianna was very active in what were then the two recognized forms of Catholic association: Saint Vincent de Paul Society and Catholic Action. She visited elderly poor people in Magenta with the Young Women of Catholic Action. They did chores, cleaned house, cooked. They also organized some very simple entertainment to which they invited these people, who in the meantime had become friends. All this, according to unanimous testimony of the participants, took place with joy and enthusiasm. Swept along by Gianna, the Young Women carried out this splendid volunteer work with joy. Even now, so many people remember those years with nostalgia and gratitude.

There was a great interior strength from the start.

Certainly. And this great interior strength was translated into enthusiasm manifested in her apostolic activity and her joy in life. My wife, for example, loved sports and played them. She played tennis, skied, climbed mountains. Another fond memory for me is dancing. Gianna could dance very well. The last time I danced with her at the Grand Hotel in Stockholm in 1961 she won the admiration of those present. She had a full, overflowing life.

Where did she get time for all these activities?

I am surprised myself when I think about it. But I must say that in all the time we lived together I never remember her idle. Even at home she knew how to organize herself marvelously. For example, she was an excellent cook. When we had guests, and friends from my company came to our house often, especially Swedes and Americans, her cooking and the way she arranged the table were greatly appreciated. In moments of calm, she mended and sewed.

Let us return to the discussion about the laity. Before the Second Vatican Council, Catholic laymen had a great many devotional practices. Can you tell us what were the devotions with which Gianna expressed her piety?

Besides daily Mass, which she hardly ever missed, was the visit to the Blessed Sacrament with some minutes of silence talking intimately with Jesus. There was daily recitation of the Rosary. As a young man, I recited the Rosary too, but she had a diligence and constancy that I lacked.

And meditation?

Reading her writings, there is confirmation that as a young woman she gave it great importance. From the time we were married, Gianna would spend a few minutes of recollection and meditation in the chapel at Ponte Nuovo. Silence was very important for her too.

My impression is that silence is important for the family, not just for spiritual life.

Certainly, it is easier for wisdom to emerge in silence, for a veil of peace and serenity to be placed upon family problems.

What is PAS?

"PAS" stands for Prayer, Action, and Sacrifice. It was the motto and the apostolic watchword for members of Catholic Action, and Gianna made it her own.

We have already recalled that prayer was irreplaceable for her. Besides Gianna was very attentive and did not do things by halves. She committed herself to her duties completely. She had also been formed by loving sacrifice and demonstrated that she knew how to sacrifice herself for love. Gianna was a woman of few words who avoided gossip and silliness on principle. This is a family virtue— her brothers and sisters don't like to talk a lot. However, when there was something to do, a service to perform, a hand to lend, then Gianna was always ready, available.

What was Gianna's relationship with the priests with whom she worked as a laywoman?

In her youth, Gianna worked with Monsignor Righetti at Genoa Quinto and then at Magenta with Monsignor Luigi Crespi both in Catholic Action and in the Saint

Vincent de Paul Society. After marriage, she also worked with Father Agostino Cerri. Monsignor Righetti, Monsignor Luigi Crespi, and Father Agostino Cerri were all very open priests who had many initiatives. It seems to me that Gianna had a frank relationship of mutual esteem and real respect with these priests. She was fortunate to have found them. Of course, two of her brothers were priests, and she was particularly proud of them.

CHAPTER THREE

MEDICINE

How did your wife choose the medical profession?

I met Gianna when she was already a physician. So to answer your question, I have to refer to testimony of relatives. They report that Gianna chose medicine in the belief that more than other professions, it would permit her to help many people in body and spirit. Besides, this profession is based on interpersonal relationships, to which Gianna was much inclined. In her manuscripts she says precisely that a doctor has opportunities closed even to the priest. In her view, a doctor has to care not only for the body, but also for the soul. Thus, she conceived the profession as a mission. Besides, I can testify to the great affection that her patients had for her, an affection that endures to this day. Service to one's neighbor was a very strong ideal in the Beretta home. For Gianna, the choice of medicine also meant continuing her commitment to the service of neighbor, as she had learned in her family and had done in the apostolate with young women in Catholic Action.

Besides, the study of medicine was a family tradition.

Yes, she had an uncle who was a physician and two brothers who studied medicine. However Gianna was not the sort to uncritically follow a general direction.

Can you tell us about your wife as a doctor?

As I already related, I first met Gianna dressed as a doctor at the Magenta Hospital and as a colleague of her brother Nando [Fernando]. In 1950 he opened an office for INAM (Istituto Nazionale Assistenza Medica) patients at Mesoro, four kilometers north of Magenta, where the municipal doctor was unable to meet all the demands. Gianna quickly became familiar to everybody with her Fiat Cinquecento, which reached even the most isolated farms farthest from the center of town. Soon she became an indispensable presence, to whom mothers, young women, the old, and the poor turned. She specialized in pediatrics in 1952 and, right after our marriage, accepted the post of health director of a day-care center and a maternity center, both directed by the Opera Nazionale Maternità e Infanzia. At the same time, Gianna donated her services as school physician for the children in the nursery school run by the Canossian Sisters and the elementary school, both at Ponte Nuovo de Magenta. How many children Gianna took care of, and how many mothers she encouraged and consoled! This explains the great affection that people there had and still have for her.

So, your wife was a general practitioner and a pediatrician at the same time?

Yes, to the end she continued to also practice general medicine. In particular, she had a predilection for the elderly, whom she loved to visit at home, even without being called.

There is a teaching about medicine, which is very important in my opinion: there must be respect for the body, which is also respect for the patient. Before making proclamations about health reform, about different kinds of medicine, my impression is that we should begin with respect for the body, which becomes respect for the person of the patient.

Gianna had a holy respect for the body and the person of the patient. Holding a concept frequently expressed in the Church's preaching and shared by many believers, she almost venerated the human body. She often repeated: "Whoever touches the body of a patient, touches the body of Christ." It was a quasi-sacramental concept, according to which Gianna sought to cure illnesses but at the same time bring comfort to spirits. The sick realized they were treated with dignity and were grateful. This, I believe, was the source of the people of Mesero's great affection for Gianna. I can find no other explanation.

Thus she overcame the distance, the dependence of the patient on the doctor.

Certainly, in her profession Gianna behaved as a friend; toward mothers she acted as an older sister, a kind sister who gave advice.

This is a lesson about faith but also a profoundly human rule, as Pius XII taught at the time in his famous speeches to physicians.

That is true. Gianna's behavior was deeply human. The people she attended in Mesero, many of whom are still alive, affirmed it and still affirm it, and along with them the mothers of Ponte Nuovo.

Let me briefly underline this aspect: medicine is a kind of image of Christian reality. Both are pure service. They fail their proper vocation if they are closed in themselves. Therefore, a true physician is both a human and Christian model.

In this sense Gianna was a true doctor and wanted to go on even after marriage. Already during our engagement, Gianna had asked me about continuing her profession at least as long as her obligations as wife and above all as mother allowed it. I did not oppose that because I knew well how enthusiastically she practiced medicine, how attached she was to her patients. Later, by mutual agreement, we made the decision that she would stop at the birth of our fourth child. In this understanding, she continued her profession until her last confinement.

BEAUTY OF THE PHYSICIAN'S MISSION

In some way, every one of us works in the service of men. We work directly upon men. The object of our science and work is man, who in our presence tells us about himself, "Help me", and hopes for the fullness of his existence from us.

Jesus would say to us: What is a person? A person is not only body. In that body there is thought, a will, which is capable of meeting suffering, which could not happen otherwise. In the body there is a spirit, and as such it is immortal. There is an abyss between body and soul; they are two very different entities, but they are united. What would Jesus say to you? You should take every care of this body. God has so inserted the divine in the human that everything we do assumes greater value.

Today, unfortunately, there is too much superficiality even in our work. We care for bodies but often without competence.

1. Do our part well. Study your sciences well. There is a race for money today.

2. Let us be honest. Be trustworthy physicians.

3. Take affectionate care, thinking that they are our brothers. Act with delicacy.

4. Do not forget the sick person's soul. Given that we have the right to certain confidences, be careful not to profane the soul. It would be a betrayal. Be careful about superficial remarks, about how we instinctively tend to treat chastity, when chastity is really strength and firmness.

Rather do *good*. We have opportunities that a priest does not. Our mission is not ended when medicines are of no more use. There is the soul to take to God, and your word will have authority. Every physician should deliver a patient to the priest. These Catholic doctors, how necessary they are!

The great mystery of man—he has a body but also is supernatural soul—is Jesus: "Whoever visits the sick, helps me." Priestly mission: as the priest can touch Jesus, so we touch Jesus in the bodies of our patients —poor, young, old, children.

May Jesus be able to make himself seen through us; may he find many physicians who offer themselves for him: "When you have finished your profession—

if you have done that—come to enjoy the life of God, because I was sick, and you healed me."

> — *Writings of Gianna Beretta Molla.*
> *Transcription of page 27 of the manuscript pad*

Saint Gianna's office [2004]

CHAPTER FOUR

WOMAN AND MOTHER

The tenderness of Gianna's letters has struck me. Perhaps this is why your wife is fascinating. In a world that sometimes is in danger of being rude, hurried, and superficial, the letters, rich in affection and tenderness, seem to bring an important message. We have to find the strength to tell about her tenderness, without being afraid of using diminutives, pet names, comparisons with nature.

You are right. Indeed, at the beginning of our engagement, I suddenly found myself confronted with this young woman who began by telling me: "I want to make you happy; tell me what I should do to make you happy." And this woman full of joy and tenderness was extremely good to me.

There was the tenderness of an accomplished woman who translated her love for life into intensity, giving depth to daily life. Particularly in this, she has been my teacher. In fact, I had received a religious formation that by today's standards could be judged too rigid, a little sad, and perhaps marked by too many prohibitions. With Gianna I entered an atmosphere of spiritual serenity, of faith lived with joy, in which all things are good and pure when they are done with a pure heart.

Perhaps a young person needs to have courage to react to beauty,
even to set in writing the feelings it provokes and to cultivate our
memory of them.

Gianna had that courage and found true beauty in living
with joy and love in the grace of God, "with Jesus in
her heart", in admiring and enjoying the wonders of creation, in seeing the gift of God everywhere in the relation
of respect and love with the creatures of God. Not only
that, but she also had the courage to put these feelings in
writing. Writing fixes and conserves states of mind and
perceptions. Words, by contrast, leave only a trace, which
is diluted with time. Then, there is the issue of youth continued, protracted. To reread letters written in the happy
period of falling in love gives a very sweet memory of
relived youth. Gianna kept my letters in a little coffer
that she received as a wedding gift. For my part, I did the
same, and rereading them now, I still seem to hear her
voice and relive the same sentiments, the same joy.

With reference to the theme of womanhood, it seems to me that
there is a special beauty in maternity. From this point of view
your wife seems to me a very beautiful mother.

Certainly, so many virtues come together to make mothers good and beautiful, and it is the sum of these virtues
that are disclosed in the faces, the eyes, and the smiles of
mothers and makes their beauty stand out. In Gianna's
case, her serenity, the harmony of her emotions, the grace,
the intensity, and the joy of her maternal love shone
through on her happy mother's face. I would add that
Gianna took care of herself, her appearance, her clothes.

Certainly, the basis of her beauty as a mother was in her clean and good conscience, emanating from her trust in Providence, but it seems important to me also that she was concerned about herself, her appearance.

So Gianna was beautiful even in ordinary family life?

Yes, she was—in her affection, in her energy, in attentiveness to the children and to me, in simplicity of manner, in care for herself, in knowing how to balance duty and joy for life, religious practice and time for concerts, theater, skiing: to sum up, in her typically feminine ability to know how to fulfill herself completely and harmoniously. So, in our workaday life, Gianna introduced the elements of beauty and festivity.

Something many people acknowledge about Gianna was her way of presenting herself, the charm with which she engaged people and situations. What is your recollection?

Gianna's deportment was marked with responsibility and kindness, with a smile, and, at the same time, she quickly inspired sympathy and trust. This deportment was still more admirable because it went along with a firm character and strong personality. She was able to make herself respected as a professional without ever losing sensitivity, charm, a kind of attractive feminine dignity.

In fact I don't believe that the emotion with which her patients recall her and are grateful to her are due only to her ability as a physician, to her availability. I think this recognition goes to a mother's and friend's tenderness, to a woman's charm, which is a reflection of interior grace,

HYMN TO THE SMILE

To smile at God, from whom all gifts come to us.

To smile to God, the Father, with ever more perfect prayers to the Holy Spirit.

To smile at Jesus, drawing near him in Holy Mass, in Communion, in visits to the Blessed Sacrament.

To smile at him who personifies Christ, the Pope; at him who personifies God, our confessor, even when he calls us to mortification.

To smile at the Holy Virgin, model upon which we must pattern our lives, so that whoever looks at us may be led to good thoughts.

To smile at the guardian angel because he was given us by God to guide us to paradise.

To smile at parents, brothers, and sisters, because we ought to be torches of joy, even when they impose duties on us that go against our pride.

To smile always, pardoning offenses.

To smile in the Association, banishing any criticism and murmuring.

To smile at those whom the Lord sends us during the day.

The world seeks joy but does not find it because it is far from God.

We, full of the joy that comes from Jesus, carry joy in our hearts with Jesus. He will be the strength that helps us.

— *Writings of Gianna Beretta Molla*
Notebooks of Recollections, nos. 6–7

of grace given by God. In her writings Gianna very much insists on living in grace and transmitting grace. I believe she lived this program fully. That is also the prevailing recollection in testimonies of friends. Father Gotti, a family friend, was a guest for three days in our house at Courmayeur. In thanking us, he stressed Gianna's sensitivity, her ability to discover the needs of others, the wishes of others.

You fell in love with Gianna. Can you tell us what attracted you most?

During our engagement, her enthusiasm and her joy. When we were married, her maternal love, her fortitude, and her joy again. This is perhaps the characteristic that struck me most. Gianna's life was a hymn to joy, a hymn to be happy with the grace of God in our hearts. Among her writings there is one entitled "Hymn to the Smile", which I think is worth reading.

Did your wife nurse the children herself?

Yes, she nursed them as long as her milk let her.

I was thinking about the image used by the prophet Isaiah in which God's fondness for his people is compared to that of a mother for her child (see Is 66:10–13). You could almost say that God takes lessons from mothers.

I also think that the love of a mother for her own children is the most similar in intensity and sweetness to God's love for his people. That doesn't surprise me because the

mother is closest to God in participation in the mystery
and marvel of creation.

In pictures taken of Gianna, her face is most beautifully
sweet, luminous, and joyful in those where she has her
babies in her arms.

What kind of education did you want to provide for your children?

The type of education Gianna proposed to me was the one
she grew up with: education by persuasion. She would
say: "I can't conceive of a mother slapping a child. We
ought to manage to educate them by persuasion and above
all educate them, from the earliest years, to see a gift of
God in everything and to respect this gift." When Gianna proposed that model of education, I was in complete agreement. I also, in fact, had the luck to have parents who educated me with persuasion.

Probably I am getting away from your question now,
but when I speak of my parents, I spontaneously come to
thank God for having given them to me, and, especially,
I thank him for my wonderful Papa, who taught me always to respect people. This teaching was invaluable and
decisive for my life. So, we were in full agreement about
the type of education for our children. Sadly, Gianna died
when Pierluigi, our firstborn, was five years old, so that
the education of our children was still in its first steps.

*You show us a beautiful life, a joyful life, but you two also had
difficulties.*

Certainly. Gianna was a wise and practical woman. From
the time of our engagement, she urged me to be ready to

overcome difficulties we might encounter. Among such difficulties I remember especially physical suffering. Gianna suffered a great deal during all her pregnancies. How much she really suffered, I learned only after her death, because she hid it from me carefully. I knew about vomiting, about stomach acidity, but not about other suffering. Also, I remember the difficulty of living in a house on the grounds of the factory I directed. It was a nice house, but it was always in the factory. Furthermore, during the two-year period from 1956 to 1958, when there were major strikes, with demonstrations that were audible from our house, and with me in the midst of the workmen. Gianna faced these difficulties without ever complaining. This strength also won her general respect and sympathy.

*Saint Gianna, Mariolina, and Pierluigi
in their home at Ponte Nuovo, 1958*

CHAPTER FIVE

NO GREATER LOVE

Your wife loved children very much. Can you tell us how she showed this love?

It showed in special predilection, in tenderness, and in the affection and intensity of her care. Shortly after our marriage, I saw proof in the enthusiasm and joy with which she accepted the appointment as health director of the day-care center at Ponte Nuovo di Magenta and as school physician for the nursery and elementary schools, also at Ponte Nuovo. Then, too, her great love for children was what made her want to have a large family of her own.

Have you seen her take care of the children at her work?

Yes. Dozens of times I saw her at work and could admire her delicacy, her attentions, her affection. It was a mother's affection, that of a woman who had enthusiastically embraced the vocations to motherhood and the medical profession.

Besides, during her high-school years, Gianna had been the delegate for the youngest girls in Catholic Action. It seems to me that this is also a sign that shows her love for children.

Naturally, afterward, love for children became love for her own children.

Yes, our children were her delight, her pride, her treasures, as she loved to repeat. For them, with them, her joy was full and perfect.

If she loved children so much, Gianna's choice to die to have another child has all the more significance.

Hers is certainly a heroic testimony of maternal love. Her choice of love was extremely difficult for a mother who loved her three other children intensely and loved life itself.

It was a choice that could be understood and properly valued only in the light of Gianna's firm convictions, her conscience as a mother, her unshaken trust in Providence. Gianna was firmly convinced that the baby she was carrying was someone to love, to respect, and not an object about which she might exercise her own preference.

It was certainly a dramatic choice. The more I think about it, the more I realize that it must have been a tremendous sacrifice for this woman. In any case, it was a cruel dilemma: either sacrifice the baby or give her own life with the consequence of leaving four children motherless, a choice to which many object. I don't feel up to saying anything except to underline Gianna's trust in Providence.

Do you still remember those moments of great suffering?

Not only do I remember, but many times I live them as if it were now. I still see Gianna, on Easter morning

1962, in the maternity section of the Monza Hospital, as she picks up the baby with great effort, lifts her and kisses her, looking with sadness and suffering that prove to me she was aware that she was going to leave her an orphan. From that day, her sufferings never ceased. She called on her mother to be near and help her, because she could not manage, the pain was so great. It seemed to be a slow, dramatic sacrifice, which accompanied Christ on the Cross. The suffering increased more on Monday. I tried to be with her constantly. I slept at Monza, in my old school of San Giuseppe. Then, fortunately, her sister Mother Virginia arrived from India and did not leave her. In the night between Easter Tuesday and Wednesday, she had a serious collapse. Wednesday morning she recovered a little and said to me: "Pietro, I was already over there and do you know what I saw? Some day I will tell you. But because we were so happy, we were too comfortable with our marvelous babies, full of health and grace, with all the blessings of heaven, they sent me down here, to suffer still, because it is not right to come to the Lord without enough suffering." This was the last exchange with my wife. Afterward, she still said a few words, but, for me, this was her testament of joy and suffering, of dedication and trust in God.

Again, I emphasize that it was trust in God and his providence that gave Gianna the courage to make that choice of love that cost her life. But one must not believe it was easy to accept the mystery of pain. Here indeed, we touch that mystery.

The mystery of pain has touched you too.

Yes. It touched me in September 1961, when Gianna was diagnosed with a miofibroma in the uterus during her second month of pregnancy. It seized me before her operation when Gianna made the firm request that her pregnancy be saved, even at the risk of her life. It lived with me in the seven months before the birth. It became worse a few days before the birth when Gianna, facing the dilemma of saving herself or the baby in her womb, firmly requested that the baby be saved. It oppressed me in the week of Gianna's Calvary after the birth. I clung to faith, to prayer, to Providence. I refused to think that Gianna would die.

When the mystery of pain came down on me and my children after Gianna's death and I felt myself crumble, I clung to Jesus crucified, to the certainty that Gianna lived with God in paradise.

A passage from a Dominican Father's sermon that I heard on Corpus Christi 1950 kept pounding at my mind: "The Eucharist is a great gift, a mystery, but the true mystery for man is pain." Besides, the Eucharist also springs from pain and death.

Think of our hospitals, to which sometimes we give only a distracted glance. There, we have whole cities of men and women who suffer, of children who die. What a great mystery!

Then, there is the insidious question: there are people who could be saved but still die. Gianna could have been saved; her illness was not incurable, but she died. I relived this mystery of pain in an equally dramatic way when my daughter Mariolina died.[1] Why does it happen?

Nobody has been able to respond to Job's "why?" except Jesus Christ on the Cross. The Son of God invites us to climb onto the Cross with him and to descend to the tomb afterward.

I confess that for a long time I looked for an explanation for why the Lord had not accepted my supplications and those of my family and so very many others that Gianna's life be saved together with that of the baby she had borne. A first light for my sorrowful search came from Cardinal Giovanni Colombo when, at the ceremony of naming the Ponte Nuovo elementary schools after Gianna on September 24, 1966, he said: "Faced with such a shining example, which cannot be forgotten by the Church, our desire is to be silent, to meditate, to admire, to pray; and into our hearts comes a desire to make ourselves

---

[1] Gianna and Pietro Molla's second child, Mariolina, was a boarder at the Sorriso d'Italia School, headed by Pietro Molla's sister, Sister Luigia at Imperia. At the beginning of 1964, she contracted particularly virulent exanthema. Other complications occurred, making it necessary to transport the child from the Imperia Hospital to the Niguarda Hospital at Milan. Unfortunately, the Milanese physicians were unable to save her.

Her father recalled her, in *Terra ambrosiana*, pp. 42–43: "Not two years had gone by when the mystery of pain and death visited our house again. Our gentle, good Mariolina joined you in Paradise. She was not yet seven. Since then I invoke her as a gentle protector and turn to her when I feel tired. We had hardly arrived from the Imperia Hospital to the Niguarda Hospital in Milan, when she affectionately directed her last words to me: 'Go home, Papa, you're tired.' A few hours later she died, praying the Hail Mary."

worthy of *this soul the Lord sent to earth undoubtedly to bring a message.* He has said that there is no love greater than that which gives its life for the beloved." Gianna had the courage to take the path of this greater love and was able to imitate the redemptive sacrifice of the Lord Jesus more closely.

I have been forced to conclude that pain remains a mystery even in the light of our faith, and I have experienced in myself that the only way to accept it is that of Jesus crucified. Now I realize that Gianna's life, her testimony, her sacrifice fit a plan of God. There is a passage in her notes for the conferences to Young Women of Catholic Action that strikes me in a particular way, makes me meditate, and seems like a presage: "Love and sacrifice are as intimately connected as sun and light. We cannot love without suffering or suffer without loving. Look how many sacrifices are made by mothers who truly love their children. They are ready for everything, even to give their own blood. Did not Jesus die on the Cross for us, out of love for us? Love is affirmed and confirmed with the blood of sacrifice."

After her death you had to think immediately about the children, particularly the newborn.

When Gianna died I had to make a great effort not to let myself be beaten down by the weight of responsibilities and duties to our children left motherless so early. I prayed so much to Gianna to watch over us, to protect us, to help us. I experienced her watching over us and helping us greatly. Gianna's relatives and mine were most generous and available. The newborn was immediately the object of particularly affectionate care. Thank God, my children grew up honoring the memory and witness of their mother.

The children also forced you to look forward.

Yes, their simple faith, surer than mine, left me no escape: "If Mamma is in heaven, why are you crying?" As we left the funeral Mass, the oldest, five and a half years old, asked me: "Does Mamma still see me, still hear me, still touch me?" Later: "Does Mamma still think about me?" I gave a hurried Yes four times and asked Jesus to give me the same certainty. Being so little, the children helped me very much; they have been a great push to go on with life.

Did you ever think of marrying again?

No. Sincerely. We loved each other too much, and for me Gianna was a wife and mother without equal.

So you experienced death, but then faith made you turn your gaze toward resurrection . . . ?

. . . faith and trust in Jesus—the way, truth, and life. I have a memory that has kept me company all these years. With Gianna, I went to the Sant'Erasmo Theater to see Diego Fabbri's *Processo a Gesù*. In the play there are many characters who laugh at Jesus. But there is a mother who has lost her son who says: "Leave me this Jesus, leave him to me, because he gives me the security that my son still lives and waits for me in paradise." So, Jesus is the one who has given security to me, and I have held on to him with all my strength.

LEAVE ME JESUS

The little woman: Wait a moment. Because I too want to say what the lady there already said . . . and the young man. You should leave Jesus alone. We are not intelligent enough to spend whole days reasoning. . . . We are poor . . . and simple, and we feel for Jesus, we know him, if you'll excuse me, as if he were one of us. He is our treasure. So you must not take away the only thing we have, which is everything for us. Jesus is everything for us! Oh, I am a mother; I work here, in the theater —I sweep . . . I clean up—oh! I get a couple of dollars and they give me a room to live in. . . .

Hey! I'm a mother with a dead son, I wanted to say. A widow . . .

My son went away, too, one fine day. . . . Children, good and bad, all go away. . . . It is destiny. . . .

Then they send me a letter: that he died. I couldn't believe it. . . . I thought I'd go crazy. . . . He isn't there anymore. . . . Yet I hear him speak, he who never spoke to me. . . . I finally hear him call—oh! gentleman of the court, earlier you spoke of miracles—I heard: they exist, they do not exist, they are true, they are false . . . a big argument . . . then the gentlemen in the armchairs: another discussion . . . I don't know if I understand, but I can say that a real miracle happened to me. I said before that from a certain point on my son became a stranger to me—but, lo and behold, after he died, after they killed him, he suddenly came back to life. . . . He came back to life inside of me. I felt he was near, alive—just as if he were alive and confided

in his mother. . . . He talks, says what he never said
for years—marvelous things . . . the words he says . . .
and the feelings he confides to me, if you only knew!
And I know now—I feel—I know it, I tell you, I do!
that not much time will go by until I see him again
—we will see each other again—because he is alive,
he's still alive. . . . It is not a fable . . . it is something
true, really true, as if you touched . . . a certainty. He
is there, in a place, in another place, and alive. He is
there, and he waits for me, and we will meet again—
and that's how it is!—I wanted to say, look . . . They
are waiting for us! These are the only things that matter
in our miserable life! So leave them alone. They are the
only things we have. . . . Be good, judges, be a little
bit good toward the Savior.

— Diego Fabbri, *Processo a Gesù*, Part II (Trial of Jesus.
English version titled *Between Two Thieves*).

*Let me say that Blessed Gianna Beretta performed the first mir-
acle with you, keeping you together, being close to you, helping
you to overcome such a hard trial.*

Yes, Gianna has been really so close to me and the children. When I think of the trials I had to overcome, I can't
explain it without direct help from Gianna.

I don't know if we can talk about a miracle. But I
have always felt her so close. To give an example, as an
engineer, I still feel a thrill when I pick up the phone
and someone from Buenos Aires answers. I think of my
uncles who migrated to that country, where they arrived

after a two-month voyage without our being able to hear
their voices ever again. Science has shown us different
forms of presence. I will say more: it ought to be easier
for us to believe. My grandparents and my parents had to
make a great effort to believe in the truth of those verses
in Job that say we will see God with our own eyes. Today, however, a different kind of vision is a daily reality.
We have the telephone, tape recorders, computers, television. We can see with other means, with invisible eyes.
When I was little and recited the article of the Creed
about things visible and invisible, at the time I thought
about angels. Nowadays, there are so many invisible but
present realities. They are here in this room, thousands
of magnetic, radio, and television waves that an apparatus
infinitely simpler than our brain is capable of receiving,
selecting, and ordering. Science does not lead us to matter
but to spirit. For me it follows that our loved ones can
see us, even if they no longer have eyes; they can hear us
even if they no longer have ears. Besides, if I can make a
theological consideration, I would like to observe that if
our beloved are in God, they are where God is present,
that is, according to the catechism, in heaven, on earth,
and everywhere. I have had proof of this in so many circumstances, in difficulties. Gianna follows me, hears me,
heeds my calls for help.

CHAPTER SIX

BEATIFICATION

Who first began to speak about Gianna's sainthood?

When Gianna died in 1962, I received many demonstrations of sympathy. Many were the ordinary expressions of condolence. Others, however, were different, because they expressed hope. They spoke of Gianna's great love, of her love for others, of her dedication to the will of God. Then the month after she died, Father Alberto, her missionary brother, wrote from Brazil: "We weep, but all paradise is joyful to see such a shining star arrive up there so close to God. . . . This evening, rather than offering the seventh-day Holy Mass for her, I would like to celebrate the Mass of the Angels; but our prayers, which we always have an obligation to say, will help so many others who need them."

A year later in 1963, Father Olinto Marella, our friend who attended Gianna during her last week, wrote and printed a pamphlet. Though careful to respect Church legislation, the pamphlet declared he was convinced of Gianna's sanctity. I should say that at the time I begged Father Marella not to give too much publicity or wide circulation to the pamphlet. On Christmas Eve in 1962, the province of Milan awarded a gold medal in Gianna's memory. It was a secular ceremony, but the Archbishop of Milan, Cardinal Montini, who a few months later was elected Pope, was present. He was aware of Gianna's sacrifice and from then on followed with interest, although with his customary discretion, the path which has led to beatification.

When did the actual process of beatification start?

In spring 1970, Bishop Carlo Colombo came to my parish in Ponte Nuovo di Magenta to administer confirmation. He told me of the Church's desire—eight years had already passed since Gianna's death—to promote the cause of my wife's beatification and requested my approval. I was very surprised! I had never heard of a mother becoming a saint. "Think it through carefully", I told him. "I did not realize that I lived with a saint."

My reticence came from my immediate understanding that this meant making our lives, our affections, our sufferings public. Gianna's decision, her sacrifice, would be proposed as a model. Some mothers would be able to understand her sacrifice, while others would think it had been exhibitionism, almost a provocation. Then, too, I was afraid of the press: we have always been a little reserved. So, I was perplexed. My conversation with the Bishop lasted for about an hour. He, as I recall, referred to Pope Paul VI's interest. He went on to affirm that Gianna's example might be a point of reference for so many mothers, for families in general. At that time, I could not ask for my children's agreement because they were too little. So, I had to decide alone; and despite the considerations I have mentioned, I gave a favorable response. I was particularly struck by Bishop Colombo's reflection that Gianna's witness could do so much good. How could I deny this request when Gianna had been so generous? A negative reply seemed to be in glaring contrast with that thirst for apostolate, with that will to do good to others, to help the elderly and needy, that Gianna had always shown in her life. So I replied positively, but requested that the process should not last too long so as to avoid placing my children under too much stress.

From that moment, however, you yourself have reexamined your wife's life.

I have reexamined my wife's life; and thanks to the diligence of Monsignor Antonio Rimoldi, who was in charge of the official biography, I have also been able to read Gianna's writings, with which I previously had not been acquainted. In fact, she had not brought these writings to our home, but had left them in the family home in Magenta. Not only that, but in her habitual discretion, not wanting to let the right hand know what the left hand was doing, she never spoke to me about the degree of her involvement in Catholic volunteer work. Therefore, thanks to the process, I have been able to review Gianna's life. I have been able to know her writings, which are very important to understand her human and religious personality. In fact, from these notes, which are an outline for the meetings with the young women of Catholic Action, we know her vision of grace, of joy, of prayer, of the importance of meditation, of retreats. In Gianna's reflections about vocation, marriage, love, sacrifice, about the unbreakable link between love and sacrifice, an inner world is revealed that has let even me know her spiritual depth and comprehend previously unknown motivations.

Have you not had the sensation of being obliged to give up your wife again, of making her available to everyone in—excuse the expression—a second sacrifice?

Really, that is precisely the way I felt so many times. And it is what our youngest child, Gianna Emanuela, has experienced because she has been the most pressured emotionally. On the other hand, our gift has been generously rewarded with the sympathy and warmth of so many people who have taken pains to let us know their feelings and to whom we are very grateful. Equally, we are grateful to the Church, which conducted the process of beatification with a rapidity that we did not dare hope for. It declared Gianna blessed in the Year of the Family, and it proposed her precisely as a model for mothers. Furthermore, there is a theme that recurs in letters from so many mothers that I receive from Italy and from abroad: many letters and publications from Germany talk about *Mutter* Gianna. All those mothers write that they turn to the intercession of Gianna because as a mother she must have faced their same problems and so is able to understand them and help them.

What has been your children's attitude as they grew up?

For the children, especially for Gianna Emanuela, the process of beatification has been rather painful.

Especially the beginning, they would have preferred

that our vicissitudes had been kept within the family. They did not enjoy the publicity that surrounded us, that newspapers and magazines spoke about their mother. Then, gradually, little by little as the process went on, we spoke, and I managed to explain things. I told them: "Children, I didn't want the process of beatification. I could have vetoed it when they sought my permission, but I consented to it because I was assured—as you too can see—that Mamma's witness can do good to so many people. In life, Mamma always tried to do good to all she met, so it was not right to say no. It is a sacrifice that we must make together. Our sacrifice is insignificant beside Mamma's." Gradually, they understood, and they have followed attentively and with great emotion the completion of the diocesan process in Milan in 1986 and the ceremony of beatification at Rome in 1994. The last child, Gianna Emanuela, was the one who suffered most. They tortured her over the telephone and recorded her answers. Sometimes she would tell me: "Papa, I can't stand it any more. I am going to some solitary place where I hope no one will ever find me." It has not been easy for Gianna Emanuela to go through these trials. But, in any case, she has come a long way. Now sometimes she comes with me to the celebrations in honor of her mother, and she is moved even more than I by the veneration and devotion for Gianna.

Has Gianna's family been favorable to the cause of beatification? Have they helped it?

Yes, very favorable and very helpful, especially Father Alberto. Before becoming ill, he was very active. When

Monsignor Colombo proposed that we gather prelimi-
nary testimony for the informative process, it was precisely Father Alberto who carried out this task when he
came from Brazil to Italy on vacation.

I FEEL LIKE A MEMBER OF
AN EVER LARGER FAMILY

It was hard for me to discover one day that I was the
daughter of a beatified mother. It still is. Hard, because
within me intense feelings that can't be put into words,
of joy, admiration, honor, and pride alternated with a
great fear of not being worthy of her and a sense of
deep responsibility.

Since last April I feel like a member of an ever larger
family, composed of all who pray to Mamma with me,
who confide in her, and feel her beside them as an example to imitate, and I experience the extraordinary sensation of never feeling alone. Within me I feel strength
and courage to live; I feel that life smiles at me, encour-
aging me in my natural tendency to honor the memory
of my mother and make her proud of me by dedicating
my life to attend and care for the elderly, her favorite
patients. I believe she will be happy with that.

— *Testimony of Gianna Emanuela Molla*
reproduced by Italia sud, *nos. 9/10 (1994), p. 15*

---

*In Father Alberto's hospital in Brazil the official miracle for the
beatification was confirmed.*

Yes. There is an officially recognized miracle, although
now many people declare they owe their cure or spiritual

peace or family harmony to Gianna. As for the official miracle, it took place in Grajaù, Brazil, at the hospital founded by Father Alberto. In October 1977, Lucia Silva Cirilo recovered from an infection that followed a Cesarean delivery of a stillborn child. The medical diagnosis was alarming. She needed to be transferred to another hospital better equipped for a dangerous operation. The doctor's worries came to the attention of a nurse, Sister Bernardina, who prayed and requested others to pray to Gianna for the woman's recovery. Against every expectation, the following day, the doctor discovered that the patient had been completely cured. She not only no longer needed an operation in another hospital, she also could go home, perfectly healed. I must say, however, that the steps to gather the documentation have been somewhat complicated. The diocese of Grajaù, in fact, had three bishops in a few years, so that more than once it was necessary to begin to gather proofs all over again. At any case, on the day of the beatification, Mrs. Cirilo was present in Rome, and it was deeply moving for me to meet her.

Will you tell us about the subsequent steps that have led to the beatification?

It is not that I have followed each step directly. Bishop Carlo Colombo provided me with the documentation, and I have been informed by Father Bernardino da Siena, postulator of the cause until December 1990, and subsequently by Father Paolino Rossi. They have been our contacts. I should also say that there has been a kind of gradual crescendo in my participation. I told you about my initial reserve. Then in 1980 when the cause was officially introduced, I began to hope, so to speak. Sometimes on a trip to Rome, going to Saint Peter's for a moment of recollection, I would think: "Maybe one day Gianna will rise to the glory of the saints. Subsequently, Father Bernardino informed us that Gianna's cause progressed rapidly, that there were no obstacles. Finally, in July 1991, there was the decree on heroicity of virtues, and in December 1992, the proclamation of the validity of the miracle.

On the latter occasion, I was invited to Rome with Father Giuseppe and Mother Virginia, Gianna's brother and sister, and Sister Luigia, my sister. On that occasion the Pope told me that Gianna is such a beautiful person, that she will do much good.

Will you tell us now about the day of April 24, 1994, the day of the beatification?

It's hard for me to put into words my state of mind and emotions on that day. Around me were my children, my little granddaughter, all the other relatives, and many, many friends. That helped me overcome the great fear of being in the first row in the immensity of Saint Peter's Square near His Holiness on live television. I found myself experiencing moments I never thought I would live to see, and for which I will never be thankful enough to the Lord, the Church, and Gianna. I must confess that for me the Mass during which Gianna was proclaimed Blessed was one long effort not to give in to emotion, not to let myself be overcome by crying. The most touching moments were when Cardinal Martini read the decree, when the Pope proclaimed her Blessed, and her tapestry was uncovered. I noted then that Gianna was truly with us. Another deeply moving moment was when we presented the gifts at the offertory. The Holy Father, recognizing me, repeated to me that Gianna was a beautiful person. Then he kissed Gianna Emanuela as if recognizing in her the mother now beatified. Receiving Communion from the Pope was also deeply moving.

The succession of feelings was incredible, to the point that now and then I had to convince myself that everything was true, that such an extraordinary event was happening to us. After Mass, we were invited to the so-called ceremony of hand kissing. In the right aisle of Saint Peter's, the Milan diocesan authorities had arranged gifts to offer the Holy Father. Cardinal Martini, other cardinals, all of the relatives, the procurator of the cause were there. During this ceremony Gianna Emanuela offered the Pope a little crown made of Gianna's rosary. The Pope accepted it with great devotion, kissed it, and then directed touching words to me. The day afterward, Cardinal Martini celebrated the first Mass in honor of Gianna at Saint Peter's. That occasion provoked a different emotion, more intimate and recollected than the day before.

On the twenty-fourth, we were in Saint Peter's Square with many people, with African rhythms and music. The next day we were inside Saint Peter's Basilica with a small group of people in great recollection. For my children and me these were moments we will never forget. After Holy Mass we went to Sala Nervi, where the Holy Father was extraordinary in the way in which he presented Gianna's testimony. Then he was particularly affectionate with us, with Gianna's relatives and children, with me. Briefly, my children and I were the objects of much attention and affection that almost seemed inexplicable and which we owe to Gianna. My daughter admitted to me: "I have never been kissed so much as that day."

Then there was a very simple episode whose significance impressed me deeply. After the morning Mass in Saint Peter's, a couple approached me. "We are engaged", they said; "we only want to tell you that after all we heard and read about Blessed Gianna, we decided to rethink the whole basis of our engagement." There, it seemed to me, that Gianna's and my marriage had a new fullness, as if we had engendered new children.

After the Roman celebrations, were there also festivities at Milan?

Certainly. On Saturday, April 30, at the cathedral, Cardinal Martini celebrated Gianna's first votive Mass within the diocese of Milan. We were touched by the great solemnity of the ritual, the homily, and the gift of the medal commemorating the beatification with an inscription composed by him, which pleased me very much: "Marvelous woman, lover of life, mother, physician, exemplary professional, she offered her life to avoid violating the mystery of the dignity of life."

Furthermore, on the evening of May 20 at Mesero, Cardinal Martini in person presided over a celebration of praise and thanksgiving, blessing a square named for Gianna and a marble plaque on the façade of her health center, rendering homage at Gianna's tomb and moving everyone with his homily. I must say that when I think about how Cardinal Martini, the organizing committee, and the diocese of Milan prepared, participated, and celebrated Gianna's beatification, I can't help thinking that they could not have done better or more than they did. For that, my children, Gianna's brothers and sisters, and I are profoundly grateful.

Who is Gianna for you now?

On the one hand she is still that sweet creature with whom I had the grace of living for seven years. She is my wife, mother of my children. On the other hand, she is the mother of many others. Many others feel she is their mother and friend, and given the Church's recognition, I also feel I should kneel before her. But, to be sincere, she is still my Gianna. Here is a recent episode. The other day I was at Reggio Emilia for a testimony about Gianna, and I went to greet the Bishop, who told me, joking: "Molla, you're unique. When a man and a woman marry, they become a single person, so that you are half in paradise already, while the other half is here with us." It was a joke, naturally. But it expresses something that I deeply feel inside.

Didn't it provoke a bit of jealousy to have to share Gianna with so many others?

I must say that initially it was rather the children who wanted to have their mother for themselves and not expose her to publicity, to indiscretion. Then little by little we learned the joy of sharing and to have big hearts from

Gianna herself. Now, even officially, Gianna is a gift for the whole Church, and we are happy when others invoke her along with us. She bears witness that such a wife, a mother can exist in this century, at the heart of the contradictions of our time. Different letters, showing great sensitivity, thank my children and me for having made Gianna's story known, for having given them such a woman, such a mother.

CHAPTER SEVEN

BLESSED [SAINT] GIANNA
AND HER CHURCH

I have the impression that your wife represents the best in Lombardy's hard-working spirit. What do you think?

Gianna was born at Magenta, but her parents lived in Piazza Risorgimento, Milan, near the Capuchin church on Viale Piave. So the Beretta couple became Franciscan tertiaries and achieved a sense of peace and joy in their faith. They transmitted the balance, peace, deep faith, frequenting of sacraments, concern for others, and love for the poor to their children. Gianna grew up with her parents' faith, and this is a great good fortune, a great gift.

Gianna and her parents certainly had the best traditional Lombard practicality and industriousness.

The Berettas were vibrant people who knew how to face difficult moments: Fascism, the war, reconstruction. The period was difficult for everybody and for them, too.

Certainly, they had to face the difficulties of big families. The Berettas had thirteen children. Six died very young, as unfortunately used to happen. So, seven were left. Still a good number, if you also think that the parents died before many of them, including Gianna, were working.

Continuing with this family atmosphere, we can say, therefore,
that when faith is authentic, it helps the believer to also be a good
citizen, a person able to see problems and to seek valid solutions.

In effect, faith helps people and makes them become still
more human, more intuitive. Gianna had the ability to
set people at ease, to understand their demands and their
needs. For me, she gave the most beautiful demonstration
of this sensitivity with the Young Women of Catholic Action. They sought out the elderly and helped them clean
house and cook. That is the understanding of faith. Besides, Gianna, although belonging to a comfortable family, had learned from her mother to cook and mend, and
she often put these talents to work.

Would you speak to us about the Geddas?

The Geddas were neighbors and friends of the Berettas
when they lived in Milan near the Viale Piave Capuchin
church. Father Alberto and Francesco, the engineer, were
good friends of Professor Luigi Gedda, while Gianna,
Mother Virginia, and especially Amalia, the older sister,
were good friends of Mary Gedda. They adhered to the
teaching of the Capuchin Father Felice da Desenzano,
whose process of beatification is in progress. He had great
spiritual influence on all of them.

However, Gedda is known as a leader of the conservative wing
of Catholic Action, whereas your wife's spirituality was more
joyful, more open.

In Gianna's time, Gedda was number one in all of Italian
Catholic Action, which seemed to me extremely serious

and active in carrying out the program "Prayer, Action, Sacrifice".

Deeply involved in that aspect of Catholic Action, Gianna knew how to live spirituality joyfully and openly, ahead of her times.

However, I can say, that the professor and his sister Mary followed Gianna's cause of beatification with great attentiveness and affection.

You often talk about Gianna's industriousness. As I was saying, it is a typically Lombardic virtue.

No doubt. On this point we were in perfect harmony with Gianna. I too had a father who gave me an example of great industriousness. When Gianna and I started a family, industriousness was immediately one of its almost hereditary characteristics, not declared but lived every day. Besides, it seems to me that this is not only a characteristic of the people, but also of the church in Lombardy. I offer only the example of Lombardic popes in this century [twentieth]: Pius XI, John XXIII, and Paul VI. They were simple and modest persons in demeanor, but extremely decisive in action.

In this Gianna was completely Lombard, and, in my opinion, this is also why the Ambrosian church and more generally the Lombard church feel so at home with Gianna.

So, there is a kind of reciprocal acknowledgment: of Gianna in the Milanese church and of the Milanese church in Gianna.

Yes, another common trait seems to me to be trust in Providence. The Lombard church, the Lombardic spirit

LET THIS SIMPLE CHARISM OF
FIDELITY TO THE GOSPEL BE SPREAD
THROUGHOUT THE WHOLE DIOCESE

Figures like Gianna Beretta Molla are a sign of hope for us, even in this confused time that we pass through, and I am convinced that by following her example, our families can be renewed and contribute to the renewal, the improvement of society.

In Gianna, in the heroism of her final moments, we acknowledge and celebrate the witness of so many other fathers and so many other mothers: fathers and mothers who have not had occasion to demonstrate their heroism, but who live their existence in silence and fidelity and form the solid fabric of our Church and of our nation.

I also think of those humble, hidden persons, whose daily fidelity is truly heroic.

By beatifying Gianna, the Church recognizes that in her it sets forth for the faithful to admire, venerate, and imitate the heroism of many parents, many mothers, many persons who honor Christ, the Church, and society in their dedicated, evangelical service. Though the conditions do not permit us to cast light on the daily activity of these persons, their heroism exists and is great.

We do not elevate Gianna to the altars as if to excuse ourselves our own mediocrity, but rather to affirm that each of us can live a fidelity that the Lord raises to sanctity.

The action of April 24 is, therefore, a powerful invitation to widespread sanctity, and the celebrations that

we will have in the diocese after the beatification will
be useful occasions to praise the Lord for our newly
beatified and for that widespread sanctity that the Holy
Spirit still diffuses today in our Church and in our families, and to pray that this simple charism of fidelity to
the gospel be diffused upon the whole diocese.

— Carlo Maria Cardinal Martini, *Meditation held
in the Basilica of Magenta, April 15, 1994*

that, for example, Alessandro Manzoni represented has
always trusted in Providence. Gianna had a very lively
trust.

Then there is a solidity in the Lombardic clergy, which
has always impressed me. People know that a Milanese
priest keeps his gaze on what is essential. They know they
can trust him, and so they do trust him.

An important characteristic is organizational talent. As
a businessman, I can admire Gianna's organizational talent, knowing how to combine so many different initiatives. Before her, I worked a lot, sometimes twelve hours
a day, and that was it. With Gianna, however, I learned
how to widen my horizons, to do other things, to find
time for culture and healthy pastimes.

*Curiously, the clergy greatly honors Gianna, the laywoman,
mother of a family. Recent popes have also been attentive and
devoted to Gianna.*

Through Cardinal Testa of Bergamo, Pope John XXIII
communicated his condolences and his admiration at

Gianna's death. I have already spoken about Pope Paul VI, who inspired the cause of beatification. His successor Pope John Paul I likewise wrote about Gianna. Lastly, Pope John Paul II has followed the cause of beatification with attention and solicitude.

And the bishops of Milan?

I have already spoken about Cardinal Giovanni Colombo. But Cardinal Martini, who is usually so measured, has also expressed enthusiasm about Gianna. Obviously, I am not an expert in causes of beatification. But I can testify that Cardinal Martini could not have done more or better for this cause. I have the impression that he took this beatification to heart. He has preached retreats in preparation, he has written for *Terra Ambrosiana* and for *L'Osservatore Romano*, he has devoted a pamphlet to the Beretta family, proposing Gianna's family as a model to lead families to pray together.

Who helps you keep Gianna's memory alive?

Her brother Father Giuseppe, who is in charge of cultural affairs for the diocese of Bergamo, was summoned often to testify about Gianna. Partly because he's a priest, I often delegate to him the task of talking about Gianna, to respond to all the questions put to me from Italy and abroad.

My impression is that over the course of the years, in the people's veneration, there have been rectifications, appropriate adjustments.

At the beginning your wife was considered as a martyr for life, then as a mother, now it seems to me that an overall consideration of her as a person has won out. What do you think?

That is true. When Gianna died, only her sacrifice was known. When Bishop Carlo Colombo sent the letter to her brother, in which he invited him to gather testimonies, the Bishop himself spoke of extraordinary sacrifice. He did not know Gianna's whole life. So, initially, they thought about the extraordinary act of a martyr. When her life was examined later, Gianna's writings were read and studied. Then they realized that Gianna's whole life was an uninterrupted act of Christian witness, of grace. Thus, this more profound understanding has led to the final picture of a woman, of a mother beatified precisely for the way in which she knew how to live every phase of her life.

That is very beautiful, because it has permitted us to enlarge our vision of Gianna's life, of her family, of the whole Milanese and Lombardic church, which produced her.

Besides, it is no accident that the first one to comprehend that Gianna is a witness with her life and not only with her final sacrifice was Monsignor Antonio Rimoldi. After having researched the official biography of Gianna by assignment of the curia of Milan, he was the one to suggest to Bishop Carlo Colombo to propose Gianna not as a martyr in defense of life, but as a witness with all her life.

A true, special popular devotion to Blessed [Saint] Gianna Beretta Molla is developing. As far as you know, where are the most active centers of this devotion?

I cannot fully answer this question. From what I can deduce from publications, from letters I receive, from invitations to testify that come to me and Father Giuseppe, the most active centers of this devotion are the diocese of Milan, different localities in other northern Italian dioceses, certain dioceses of central and southern Italy, some places in Austria, Germany, France, Portugal, Switzerland, Poland, Lithuania. In other continents, British Columbia in Canada, the United States, Brazil, Argentina, Chile, Madagascar, Thailand, India, Hong Kong . . .

Like me, Father Giuseppe Beretta, Gianna's brother, is continually invited to testify about her. Recently I have been to Matera, and the bishop told me that the first new church built in that city will be named after Gianna.

Is the conclusion of the process of canonization foreseeable? When will Blessed Gianna be proclaimed a saint?

In that regard, I know nothing definite. However, many people tell me that Gianna's witness is beautiful and contemporary, and they express the wish that she be declared a saint as soon as possible.[1]

---

[1] Gianna Molla was canonized a saint on May 16, 2004.

PART THREE

Gianna's Virtues

By Pietro Molla

Saint Gianna, Mariolina, and Pierluigi in 1958

CHAPTER ONE

LIFE IS A VIRTUE

Gianna, I gathered your writings, recollections, and testimonies. Now I want to have a conversation with you, to relive and rethink the most important moments of our life, from our first meeting in faraway 1949 to when I lost the comfort of your visible presence.

I want to tell you about the feelings, the hopes, and certainties that your life, your virtues, your heroic sacrifice still nourish.

I want to tell you about them now that they have recognized you as worthy of a cause of beatification.

I met you for the first time in my life at your brother Fernando's doctor's office in September 1949. I had gone to Fernando because I was sick. We said hello and hardly looked at each other. My first impression of you was of an extremely direct, serious person. I saw you for the second time the following year on April 16 at the Magenta Hospital, again in a white gown. You had just finished giving a blood transfusion to my sister Teresina, whom the Lord called to be among his angels a few days later. Again in that extremely painful situation, our glances hardly met.

From the testimony of Pietro Molla on the heroism of the virtues of his wife, for the beginning of the process of beatification, April 1973.

117

I had known for several years that you were a wonderful girl: medical student and then doctor, at the same time very active in Catholic Action and the Saint Vincent de Paul Conferences. I was aware of the fact that in your capacity as delegate for our zone, you periodically came to my parish at Mesero to hold conferences for the Catholic Action Young Women. On Sunday afternoons, as a student and then after graduation, I explained Christian doctrine to youths and men. I remember that the pastor, Father Giuseppe Airaghi, held you in high esteem. There was not a dissenting voice among all the people I approached, but rather unanimous appreciation for your family's and your own clear, exemplary testimony of faith and Christian life.

I met you again in the summer of 1950, when you opened the health center at Mesero and chose Mrs. Luigia Garavaglia as your nurse. She lived in my building. From the second half of 1950 to November 1954, we had some brief encounters, rapid exchanges of greetings and a half smile on occasion of your visits to the nurse, or your trips from Magenta to Mesero or mine from Mesero to Magenta. I knew how all your old and young patients unanimously appreciated and esteemed you, especially young mothers and elderly chronically ill, who derived so much comfort from your patient, affectionate, and diligent care. Everyone at Mesero knew that you cared for your patients' health competently and with very laudable effort, and, at the same time, whenever necessary, you cared for the soul, too. It was known how much good that you did with the light of the gospel for mothers and young women when they submitted maternity problems to you.

December 8, 1954, we met, when both invited to Father Lino Garavaglia's first Mass. In my diary for that day I recall you while you congratulated Father Lino and his relatives with your kind, broad, good smile. I recall how you devoutly made the sign of the cross before the meal. I also recall you in prayer at the Eucharistic blessing. I still feel our cordial handshake, and I see again the sweet, luminous smile that accompanied it.

In that radiant summer of our engagement, you were every day more that marvelous creature who gave me joy for life, for going up to mountain tops and hurtling down snowy slopes; joy in the enchantment of creation and its mysterious smile; joy at our new family, now near; joy in God's grace.

So we approached our marriage. Again, yours was the proposal to prepare ourselves with more intense prayer. September 13 you wrote me how you desired to form our family and how you perceived the sacrament of matrimony: "With the help and blessing of God we will do everything so that our new family should be a little cenacle where Jesus reigns over all our affections, desires, and actions. My Pietro, there are only a few days left, and I am so moved when I come to receive the sacrament of love. Let us become collaborators of God in creation. That way we can give him children who experience him and serve him."

How often the thought comes back to me of that sudden rumble of clapping hands when you entered the basilica of Magenta that lasted till you arrived at the altar where we were to be married. Your brother Father Giuseppe blessed our marriage and exhorted us to be witnesses to the gospel and to be saints. The fullness of our new life began for us that morning: a succession of unspeakable joys and luminous peace, of worries and suffering till that Saturday morning which saw you go up to heaven.

Your dream as a wife was to have bright and good children, many of them. Pierluigi was born, and your joy as a mother was full and perfect. It was renewed with Mariolina's birth and again with Lauretta's.

Whenever you were expecting, what prayer, what trust in Providence, what fortitude in suffering. At each birth, what a hymn of thanks to the Lord. You wanted each of our babies to be consecrated and entrusted to the special protection of Our Lady of Good Counsel immediately after the ceremony of baptism. As soon as they were old enough you wanted Pierluigi to be enrolled in Catholic Action Boys and Mariolina in the little girls' Catholic Action.

Full of joy, we observed our babies, we lived for them, and we were so proud of them.

You continued to have joy in life, to enjoy the enchantment of creation, the mountains and their snow, the symphony, and plays. At home you were always busy. I never remember you idle or even resting during the daytime, unless you were sick. Despite family obligations, you wanted to continue your mission as physician at Mesero, especially because of the affection and charity that connected you to young mothers, old people, and the chronically ill. How many affectionate cures of children from the nursery school, the day-care center, the elementary school, and at your practice for mothers at Ponte Nuovo, we saw.

Your intentions, your actions were always completely consonant with your faith, with the apostolic spirit and activity of your youth, with complete trust in Providence and with your spirit of humility. In every circumstance, you referred and trusted yourself to the Lord's will. Every day, I remember, you had your prayer and your meditation, your conversation with God, and your thanksgiving for the incredible gift of our marvelous children.

And you were very happy.

You so desired another child. You prayed and asked that the Lord would hear you. The Lord heard you, but this divine grace required the sacrifice of your life.

Many times you asked whether you were a worry to me. You said that never as then did you need tenderness and understanding.

I heard not a word from you in all those long months about your awareness as a physician of what was ahead of you. Certainly, this was to keep me from suffering.

I watched you silently tidying up every corner of our house, every drawer, every dress, every personal object day after day as if for a long trip. But I did not dare to ask myself why.

Only a few days before the birth, in a firm and at the same time peaceful tone, with a profound gaze I have never forgotten, you declared to me: "If you have to decide between me and the baby, there is to be no hesitation. Choose the baby. I demand it. Save it!"

From that moment I, too, trembled and suffered with you.

Holy Saturday morning we had the incredible joy; the divine gift of the child we awaited—Gianna Emanuela.

A few hours later, your sufferings began, extraordinary, beyond your strength, sufferings which made you continually call on your mother, who was already in heaven.

You knew you had to die, and you felt the torment of leaving all our children who were so young, but you did not admit that to me.

When you took our little infant in your arms, you looked at her so affectionately, with a look that betrayed your unspeakable suffering at not being able to look after her, to raise her, to see her again.

But even in that moment there was no hint to me that you were afraid and much less certain you had to die. Only to Sister Maria Eugenia Crippa, assigned to the gynecological division of the Monza Hospital, did you say when you entered there: "Sister, here I am; I am here to die this time." And you said it—by testimony of Sister Maria Eugenia, "with a look of sorrow for the life you regretted leaving, but at the same time with calm. A true model of heroic mother." I remember everything you said to me Wednesday morning, with such a gentle serenity that it seemed almost otherworldly: "Pietro, I'm cured now. Pietro, I was already over there and do you know what I saw? Some day I will tell you. But because we were so happy, we were too comfortable with our marvelous babies, full of health and grace, with all the blessings of heaven, they sent me down here, to suffer still, because it is not right to come to the Lord without enough suffering." This was and remains for me your testament of joy and suffering.

Then there were still greater sufferings.

You desired to receive Jesus in the Eucharist, at least

on your lips, even Thursday and Friday, when you could no longer swallow the sacred particle. Beside you was a holy priest, Father Olinto Marella.

The Lord could not attend to my weeping, my supplication, my prayers as I served Father Marella's Mass in the hospital church, holding back my tears with difficulty. He could not attend to the prayers of our babies, of that holy priest, of our many dear ones who felt anguish for your life, as if you were a member of their own family. You repeated many times in your agony: "Jesus, I love you, Jesus, I love you."

Wednesday evening you had asked to go back to our house. Saturday morning you came to your final agony.

Perhaps you, too, heard the voices of your babies, who were waking up in the next room. Almost at that very moment you went up to heaven with the saints.

*Saint Gianna with Mariolina and Pierluigi
in their garden at Ponte Nuovo, 1958*

CHAPTER TWO

THE THEOLOGICAL VIRTUES

YOUR FAITH

You absorbed your faith from your wonderful parents, both people of deep faith, and you always increased it in your family, where your upbringing was based on the sacraments and on lived Christian doctrine, as Father Felice testifies.

You received Jesus in First Communion at the age of only five and a half, and from that day for years and years, you heard Holy Mass every morning with your mother and received Jesus, your indispensable daily bread.

Educators, teachers, fellow students, from high school to the university, are unanimous in their testimony:

—Your faith did not consist of formulas but of practical, attractive witness, rendered with absolute simplicity in your actions.

—Your piety was simple yet based on profound conviction. Holy Mass for you was irreplaceable and incomparable. So you wrote in your notes for conferences for the Young Women of Catholic Action.

—You gave constant example of an intense life of piety. For example, in visits to Jesus in the Blessed Sacrament and the daily Rosary.

—Your conversation with the Lord in prayer was constant. For you it could not be replaced by any other activity, not even apostolate, as you wrote in your notes for Catholic Action conferences.

—You completely carried out Catholic Action's program concerning the Eucharist, the apostolate, and heroism. This program made you bear the responsibility of guiding the Young Women of Catholic Action to God and sanctity and made you enter their lives like a shining light.

—Your elevated Christian sense of life and virtues edified even your confessor, Monsignor Ceriani.

As soon as we met, I was aware of your clear, full faith, of how certain you were about the decisive, real necessity of an intense spirit of prayer, and of your profound piety.

To start our engagement, you were a model of clarity: "I intend to give myself to form a truly Christian family", you wrote me February 21, 1955.

In your prayers, in your daily offerings, you soon combined my work with yours, my joy and sufferings with yours.

You wanted to celebrate our official engagement with Mass and Communion, and you wanted us to prepare for our wedding with a triduum of holy Masses and Communions and prayer, certain that the Blessed Mother and Jesus would bless us.

You sought the help and blessing of the Lord so that "our new family would be a little cenacle, where Jesus might reign over our affections, desires, and actions".

Your goal of marriage was also a goal of faith. You

wrote me that on September 13, 1955: "With the sacrament of love we become God's collaborators in creation and so we can give him children that love and serve him."

In our family life, everything in you was consistent with your faith.

Every day, your prayer and meditation, your conversation with God, included the thanks for the incredible gift of our children.

You exercised your profession as a physician in complete consistency with your faith and the spirit and activity of apostolate, which in your youth and afterward too had made you active and generous in Catholic Action and in the Saint Vincent de Paul Conferences.

Your faith made you feel great satisfaction at having a brother who was a physician and Capuchin missionary, a brother who was an engineer and priest, and a sister with a medical degree who was a Canossian nun. Your faith made you desire that at least one of our children might embrace the religious life.

YOUR HOPE

The basic components of your hope were complete trust in divine Providence and in the efficacy of prayer. How often did you communicate that certainty from our first meeting until your last days!

I have never forgotten what you wrote me at the beginning of our engagement and while you were expecting our children:

—April 6, 1955: "I have so much trust in the Lord, and I am certain he will help me to be your worthy spouse."

—November 7, 1956, during the difficult pregnancy with Pierluigi: "I hope that the baby is born by the tenth of this month. I trust in Providence."

—April 29, 1957, pregnant with Mariolina: "In November Pierluigi will have a little brother or a little sister, as the Lord pleases. I am well, but as with Pierluigi, I still have nausea and vomiting, and medicines do very little for me. But it does not matter. I offer it to the Lord so that everything goes well and another handsome baby is born, healthy and lively like Pierluigi. I trust in your prayers and the graces in your *memento* during daily Mass. The Lord must hear your precious prayers."

The certainty that divine Providence predisposes and accomplishes everything for our good made you admire and appreciate more the gift of life, of families, and of creation. You truly knew how to admire joyfully and rightly the charm of mountains and their snow, trips and concerts, plays and parties.

You demonstrated to me that we can totally fulfill the Lord's will and become saints without renouncing the fullness of the best, pure joys that life and nature offer us.

Your complete trust in Providence and the certainty of the decisive efficacy of prayer gave you strength and also serenity during the last months.

When it seemed more and more probable that it was not possible to save you and the baby that you were carrying, you never despaired of Providence. You prayed that both would be saved, even as you were ready to sacrifice your life.

You loved our three children no less than you loved

the baby still in your womb. I am sure of it. For you that child had the same rights to life as Pierluigi, Mariolina, and Lauretta.

The right to life of the baby that you still had in the womb required an essential contribution from you, which in that painful situation might demand the holocaust of your life.

You knew that a mother's contribution to the upbringing, education, and formation of her children has no equal, but in your humility, and above all in the fullness of your trust in Providence, you were convinced that you were not committing an act of injustice toward our three children, because in that painful circumstance the one who had primary and indispensable need of you was the baby in your womb; and despite considering your duty to the upbringing of our children was no less serious than the duty of guaranteeing that they came to life after conception, you had complete trust in Providence regarding their education and their formation if the new pregnancy requested the sacrifice of your life.

YOUR CHARITY

Your life was a permanent act of charity, and for me the heroism of your charity was the direct consequence of the fullness of your faith and the certainty of your hope.

I know you absorbed the spirit of evangelical charity from your parents.

Everyone who knew you during your youth and your studies unanimously testified as to your charity, your love for God. You loved God and desired and acted so that many would love him. You wanted to bring souls to God, and from this came your very active apostolate in Catholic Action, your life of faith integrally lived, of intense daily prayer and activity. You felt that you loved and served God himself in your neighbor: that is why you dedicated yourself intensely and delicately to the Conferences of Saint Vincent de Paul and many other apostolates.

No wonder that this spirit and these charitable activities led you to dream, to feel yourself called to a missionary life in Brazil to help your brother Father Alberto.

The essential, dominant element of your charity was the constant, eager search for the will of God through prayer and meditation, fulfilling it day by day in any circumstance faced with difficulties, risks, and sacrifices. All who have known and appreciated you from your childhood testify to this. I can completely corroborate their testimony.

I came into your life when you understood with certainty that the will of the Lord called you to marriage and motherhood.

Your intentions, your desires, your acts were immediately in full conformity with serene trust in Providence with your spirit of humility, with your constant referring yourself and trusting yourself to the will of the Lord, with the spirit and the charitable activity of your youth, as I learned by unanimous report.

You wanted to become a spouse and mother as the Lord wished. You even wrote me about that on March 11, 1955, at the beginning of our engagement.

Truly, for you, love was what you wrote in your notes for the conferences to the Young Women in Catholic Action: "Love should be total, full, complete, governed by the law of God and ought to become eternal in heaven.''

You permeated daily life as spouse, mother, and physician, with the same spirit of love and charity of your youth.

You cared for the formation of our children and our family life with wisdom and immense affection.

AS A FLOWER THAT ADORNS THE SOUL

Charity is a theological virtue, that is, it has God for its object, like faith and hope.

With faith we orient ourselves toward God, with hope we invoke him, with charity we possess him, that is *we unite ourselves to him*. That is why charity is called the queen of theological virtues. It is that because, as Saint Paul says, while faith will have no more reason to exist in heaven because we will see God face to face, and so hope will cease because we possess God, the supreme good we hope for, charity will remain and will be the only flower that adorns the soul.

It is the root of all moral virtues, because it leads us to acquire them. How? Because if one loves a person, he repeats the acts that please the person, that bring him joy. So charity pushes the soul to the repetition of acts that please God (acts of mortification, sacrifice, avoiding evil).

It is distinctively Christian.

At the last supper Jesus said: ''By this they will know you are my disciples, if you love each other.'' Saint

Vincent de Paul said that the Christian without charity is a counterfeit Christian, not a real one.

Saint Paul: "If I speak in the tongues of men and of angels, but have not love, I am a noisy gong or a clanging cymbal. And if I have prophetic powers, and understand all mysteries and all knowledge, and if I have all faith, so as to remove mountains, but have not love, I am nothing" (1 Cor 13:1-2).

So, dear Aspirants, go on to conquer the queen of virtues—it will be a labor within us and around us—no one should fall asleep. And it must be a continual contest that will consist *of mutual help.*

— *Gianna Beretta Molla, Conference for Catholic Action Aspirants, 1945-1946*

CHAPTER THREE

THE CARDINAL VIRTUES

YOUR PRUDENCE

Special traits of your character and your conduct were equanimity, maturity, and interior purity. Before making a decision you prayed a great deal and you asked for prayers. This did not surprise me or anyone who knew you, because we all knew that you truly wanted to do only what the Lord wanted from you, and to do it completely.

YOUR JUSTICE

As models for this virtue you had your saintly parents, whom you always remembered, "so honorable and wise, with that wisdom that reflected their good and just souls in the fear of God".

Your justice led you to be understanding, sincere, affable, and patient with everyone, to give good example, to give serenity, to carry out works of apostolate, and to help the poor. For you, justice was sanctity.

You repeated to the Young Women of Catholic Action: "Sanctifying grace makes us saints, that is just."

You were just with God, and you truly felt everything as a gift of God and were always grateful to him. You were just toward our children and the family. I experienced this day by day up to your heroic justice toward the creature you had in your womb.

YOUR FORTITUDE

Fortitude was the dominant virtue in your moral life.

The testimonies are unanimous: from early youth, you strongly felt your duties, your commitments, your responsibilities in family, in studies, in Catholic Action, and in the Saint Vincent de Paul Conferences.

From high school through completion of your medical doctorate, you were laudably committed, even beyond your strength.

You suffered a great deal with disappointments and academic difficulties, but you knew how to overcome them and bear everything for the love of God. You always worked seriously, tenaciously, with the constancy of one who has accepted Christ's message.

When we met, I understood right away and you wrote it to me as well, that you wanted to be the valiant woman of Scripture. And so you were, truly. You persevered in your fortitude.

You were truly strong in suffering. You did not want your dear ones to suffer with you and for you, and you overlooked nothing so that they would not.

Your faith, your confidence in Providence, trusting yourself to the will of God, your fortitude in difficulty and suffering, your perseverance in Christian witness and charity brought you to the heroic fortitude of sacrificing your life for your child.

YOUR TEMPERANCE

You knew how to accept and appreciate the Lord's gifts, the gifts of life without ever abusing them, without ever letting yourself be overcome.

Your intentions and actions were completely consistent with your humility, with your sobriety.

You gave me the example that life and nature, music and theater, mountains and trips, love and family can be enjoyed with temperance. For you the limits of temperance were clear: the limits of the law and of the grace of God. You knew how to be disciplined; you preferred to serve than to be served.

Yet in your temperance, your balance, your interior purity knew how to find room for full and perfect joy, for a message of serenity, of joy to all you approached.

THE VIRTUE OF PERSEVERANCE

Gianna, in this conversation, I have recalled to you and to myself the most significant moments of your life, our life, your virtues and your sacrifice.

I realize that I have repeated myself more than once. When one tries to examine every theological and moral virtue, it is easy to repeat oneself, because a sentiment, an action, always are the combined result of several virtues.

There is still a virtue that is not included among the theological and moral virtues, a virtue that is seldom recalled, but that, for we humans who are called to save ourselves over a lifetime, is fundamental in this earthly life of ours: the virtue of perseverance. This was the virtue that Bishop Cesare Orsenigo, then Apostolic Nuncio in

PRAYER TO JESUS

O Jesus, I promise to submit myself to all that you allow to happen to me. Only make me know your will.

My most sweet Jesus, infinitely merciful God, most tender Father of souls and especially of the weakest, the most wretched, the sickest whom you carry with special tenderness in your divine arms, I come to you to request by the love and merits of your Sacred Heart the grace of understanding and always doing your holy will, the grace of trusting in you, the grace of resting securely for time and for eternity in your loving, divine arms.

PRAYER TO OUR LADY

O Mary, in your maternal hands I commend and abandon myself entirely, sure of obtaining what I request. I rely upon you because you are my sweet mother; I confide in you because you are Mother of Jesus; I entrust myself to you.

In this trust I rest sure of being heard in everything, with this trust in my heart I greet you *Mater mea, fiducia mea* [My mother, my confidence]; I consecrate myself entirely to you, begging you to remember that I am your own; guard me and defend me, sweet Mary, and in every instant of my life present me yourself to your Son, Jesus.

— *Gianna Beretta Molla*

Germany, recommended to me and my fellows at the Villoresi San Giuseppe School in Monza during my fourth year of high school as the most necessary for salvation and heaven. I have never forgotten it.

Truly, the Lord gave you the crown of life, mentioned in the Book of Revelation, because you have been faithful unto death, because you have persevered in virtue unto the holocaust of your earthly life.

This fidelity and perseverance in the vocation and duties of motherhood by the light of the gospel are a heroic message of faith and hope, but above all of charity, of that love which, as Saint Thérèse of the Child Jesus writes, "includes all vocations".

Gianna, may our conversation be constant too in your intercession and that of Mariolina before the Lord, so that the light of your sacrifice and of your message may dissolve the mystery of the pain of no longer having the comfort of your and Mariolina's visible presence, and may he make us persevere in virtue and grace so that one day we may join you in the crown of life without end.

Saint Gianna at Courmayeur, Northern Italy,
with Mariolina and Laura, 1960

CHRONOLOGY

October 4, 1922	Gianna is born to Alberto Beretta and Maria De Micheli Beretta in Magenta (Milan), Italy.
October 11, 1922	Gianna is baptized Giovanna Francesca in the Basilica of S. Martino in Magenta.
October 1922–1924	She lives in Milan at Piazza Risorgimento, no. 10. She attends the church at the Capuchin convent on Viale Piave.
In 1925	The family moves to Bergamo in Borgo Canale.
April 14, 1928	Gianna makes her First Communion at Santa Grata parish.
In 1928	She attends elementary school, changing schools twice. In her last years she was taught by Canossian Sisters.
June 8, 1930	Gianna is confirmed at the Bergamo Cathedral.
In 1933	She begins her studies in the gymnasium (high school) at Paola Sarpi School in Bergamo.
January 22, 1937	Gianna's sister Amalia dies at age twenty-six.
In 1937	The family moves to Genoa (Quinto al Mare) and she attends the gymnasium at the Istituto di S. Dorothea.

March 16–18, 1938	Gianna makes the Spiritual Exercises of Saint Ignatius under the direction of the Jesuit Fr. Michele Avedano at the Istituto di S. Dorothea.
1938–1939	Gianna's studies are suspended for a year for health reasons.
October 1939	Gianna begins classical studies at the Istituto di S. Dorothea, Lido d'Albaro (Genoa).
October 1941	With her family, she returns to Bergamo, to the home of her maternal grandparents at S. Vigilio. The World War II bombardment of Genoa has weakened the health of Gianna's mother, who already had heart trouble.
November 1941	Gianna returns to Genoa to finish her course of studies.
May 1, 1942	Maria, Gianna's mother, dies at age fifty-five.
June 1942	Gianna receives her diploma.
July 1942	She rejoins her family at Bergamo.
September 1, 1942	Gianna's father, Alberto, dies at age sixty.
October 1942	Gianna and her siblings move to Magenta to her paternal grandparents' home. She is involved in Catholic Action and also the Society of Saint Vincent de Paul.
November 1942	Gianna begins her studies in medicine and surgery at the University of Milan.

June 1945	Gianna continues medical studies in Padua.
September 1949	Pietro first meets Gianna at her brother Fernando's doctor's office.
November 30, 1949	Gianna receives a degree in medicine and surgery. She considers joining her brother Father Alberto, who is a missionary doctor in Brazil.
In 1950	Pietro is named central director at Saffa.
April 16, 1950	Pietro again sees Gianna (at the Magenta hospital).
July 1, 1950	Gianna opens an outpatient health center in Mesero (Milan). Pietro meets her there occasionally.
July 7, 1952	Gianna obtains her degree as a specialist in pediatrics from the University of Milan. She considers becoming a medical missionary, but because she lacks the physical health for this, her spiritual director discourages her.
December 8, 1954	Gianna and Pietro Molla begin their friendship after meeting again at the First Mass of Fr. Lino Garavaglia.
April 11, 1955	Gianna and Pietro are officially engaged.
September 24, 1955	Gianna and Pietro are married at the Basilica of S. Martino in Magenta.
In 1956	Gianna accepts an appointment as health director for a day-care center at Ponte Nuovo in Magenta.
November 19, 1956	Their first son, Pierluigi, is born at home in Ponte Nuovo.

December 11, 1957   Maria Zita (Mariolina) is born at home in Ponte Nuovo.

July 15, 1959   Laura (Lauretta) is born at home in Ponte Nuovo.

September 6, 1961   Gianna develops a uterine tumor when she is two months pregnant with their fourth child.

April 20, 1962   Good Friday. Gianna enters Monza Hospital.

April 21, 1962   Holy Saturday. In the morning Gianna Emanuela is born by Cesarean section. After some hours Gianna develops a fever and septic peritonitis, which worsens.

April 28, 1962   Gianna is returned home to her home at Ponte Nuovo, Magenta. She dies at eight o'clock in the morning.

April 30, 1962   Gianna's funeral takes place in Ponte Nuovo and she is buried at Campo Santo in Mesero.

February 12, 1964   Mariolina dies at age six.

November 6, 1972   Cardinal Giovanni Colombo and sixteen bishops of the Episcopal Conference of Lombardy petition Pope Paul VI to introduce the cause of the Servant of God Gianna Beretta Molla and begin the process of collecting information.

March 15, 1980   Pope John Paul II gives his authorization to Gianna's cause and the Congregation for the Causes of Saints grants the *nulla osta* [no obstacle].

April 28, 1980	Archbishop Carlo Maria Martini of Milan decrees the introduction of the cause.
June 30, 1980	The process is opened. It consists of 158 sessions and is not concluded until March, 1986.
April 11, 1986	The Cause of Beatification is introduced to the Congregation for the Causes of Saints.
April 12, 1986	The Decree of Opening is issued.
July 6, 1991	The Congregation for the Causes of Saints confirms and Pope John Paul II decrees that the heroic virtues of the Servant of God Gianna Beretta Molla are recognized. By this action, Gianna becomes Venerable.
March 5, 1992	The medical consultants pronounce unanimously on the validity of the miracle. During 1992 it is further examined, and on December 21, 1992 the Holy Father issues the decree of validity of the miracle.
April 24, 1994	Gianna Beretta Molla is beatified by the Holy Father, Pope John Paul II, in Saint Peter's Square.
2002–2003	The second miracle is examined and declared valid.
February 19, 2004	The process of canonization is officially concluded.
May 16, 2004	His Holiness John Paul II canonizes Gianna Beretta Molla along with five others. The ceremony takes place in Saint Peter's Square.

Mariolina, Pierluigi, Gianna Emanuela, and Laura

THE CANONIZATION

On Sunday May 16, 2004, in Saint Peter's Square, Pope John Paul II presided at the Mass of Canonization of six new saints, including Saint Gianna Beretta Molla. The Holy Father delivered his homily in Italian taking John 14:27 ("Peace I leave with you") as his text. He reminded those present that "[t]rue peace is the fruit of Christ's victory over the power of evil, sin, and death. Those who follow him faithfully become witnesses and builders of his peace."

The Holy Father spoke specifically of Gianna as follows:

Gianna Beretta Molla was a simple, but more than ever, significant messenger of divine love. In a letter to her future husband a few days before their marriage, she wrote: "*Love is the most beautiful sentiment the Lord has put into the soul of men and women*".

Following the example of Christ, who "*having loved his own . . . loved them to the end*" (Jn 13:1), this holy mother of a family remained heroically faithful to the commitment she made on the day of her marriage. The extreme sacrifice she sealed with her life testifies that only those who have the courage to give of themselves totally to God and to others are able to fulfill themselves.

Through the example of Gianna Beretta Molla, may our age rediscover the pure, chaste, and fruitful beauty of conjugal love, lived as a response to the divine call!

Reprinted from *L'Osservatore Romano*, no. 20, May 19, 2004.

APPENDIX

Prayers

"My most good Jesus, God of infinite mercy, most sweet Father of our souls and especially of the most weak, of the most miserable, of the most sick, of those souls that You carry with a special tenderness in Your divine arms, I come to ask You, thanks to the love and to the merits of Your Sacred Heart, for the grace to understand and to always do Your Holy Will, the grace to trust in You, and the grace to rest securely in time and eternity in Your divine arms filled with love."

"I make note of doing all for Jesus. I offer Him all my work, all my disappointments and sufferings. I make note that in order to serve God, I no longer wish to go to the cinema unless I know beforehand that it is worth seeing —that it is modest, moral, and not scandalous. I wish to die rather than commit mortal sin. I wish to fear mortal sin as if it were a serpent and I repeat I would die a thousand times rather than offend the Lord. I wish to ask the Lord for help not to go to hell and therefore to avoid all that would harm my soul. I will say one 'Ave' daily so that

Most of the quotations in this Appendix are taken from the booklet "Gianna Beretta Molla: Journey of Holiness", prepared under the direction of the Organizational Committee for the Beatification of Gianna Beretta Molla, trans. Sr. L. DeStefano (Milan: ITTI, 1994).

the Lord will grant me a holy death. I beg the Lord to help me understand His great mercy. I propose to obey M. M. [Mother Malatto] and to study even though I don't feel like it, for the love of Jesus. From this day on, I wish to pray on my knees in the morning in church just as I do in my room in the evening at the foot of my bed."

"Lord, keep Your grace in my heart. Live in me so that Your grace may be mine. Make it that I may bear every day some flowers and new fruit."

"Lord, may this light you have lit in my soul never be extinguished."

On Prayer

"Prayer . . . 'the soul of every apostolate', interior life, life of union with God. Constant, intense prayer to obtain grace from God. Personal and communal prayer: meditation, visits to the Blessed Sacrament, recitation of the Rosary, frequent confession, daily communion, spiritual exercises. . . ."

"Even if you go to work, don't ever neglect your meditation and if possible, make a visit to the Blessed Sacrament, receiving Communion at least once a week, if not daily. . . . Only if we are rich in grace ourselves, can we spread it around us, for we cannot give what we do not have."

"Why do you not succeed in doing good? It's because you do not pray enough."

Surrender

"Whatever God wants."

"God's Providence is in all things. It's always present."

Duty

"When one does one's own duty, one must not be concerned, because God's help will not be lacking."

"One earns Paradise with one's daily task."

"The secret of happiness is to live moment by moment and to thank God for all that He, in His goodness, sends to us day after day."

"As to the past, let us entrust it to God's Mercy, the future to Divine Providence. Our task is to live holy the present moment."

Purity

"Our body is a cenacle, a monstrance: through its crystal the world should see God."

"Purity must control the proper use of the pleasures of the senses. Our body is sacred. It is in conjunction with the soul in doing good. Purity is a resultant virtue, that is, a unity of other virtues that bring it into custody. How does one keep custody of purity? By surrounding our body with the hedge of sacrifice, purity becomes beauty. Purity becomes freedom."

Suffering and Sacrifice

"Also in suffering, let us say: Thanks be to God."

"One cannot love without suffering or suffer without loving."

"Look at the mothers who truly love their children: how many sacrifices they make for them. They are ready for everything, even to give their own blood so that their babies grow up good, healthy, and strong."

"Yes, I have prayed so much in these days. With faith and hope I have entrusted myself to the Lord. . . . I trust in God, yes; but now it is up to me to fulfill my duty as a mother. I renew to the Lord the offer of my life. I am ready for everything, to save my baby."

"Sacrifice: the final end of prayer and action is not to receive praise or self advantage but to busy oneself, as did Jesus, in the total giving of oneself for others at the cost of renunciation and suffering, in the impassionate competition of love which arrives at the sacrificing of one's own life."

"To work, to sacrifice oneself solely for the glory of God. To sow our small seed tirelessly . . . and if after having worked in the best way possible, we do not succeed, we must generously accept this. A failure well-accepted by an apostle who has used all means to succeed, is more meritorious than a triumph."

Action

"Do not be afraid to defend God, the Church, the Pope and priests. It is just the moment for action. Against this anti-religious and immoral campaign one cannot be indifferent."

"We must act, we must enter into all the fields of social, familiar and political action. And to work, because all the dark and threatening forces of evil are united. It is necessary that the forces of good be all united and form a kind of dam, a barrier as if to say: 'There is no passing over here.'"

"It is not enough to speak well, we must show by examples."

"We must be living witnesses of the beauty and grandeur of Christianity. To make truth visible in one's own person, to render truth pleasing, offering oneself as a significant and, if possible, heroic example."

"Action, Apostolate: complete dedication to others, especially for the salvation of those fallen away from the Church. All must be done for the Kingdom of God because Jesus must reign."

"Let us always work generously with humility, not wanting to see immediate results in our work. That which counts is to work and not to give up. Saving the world has never been an easy task, either for the Son of God or for the Apostles. I have told you that Catholic Action is sacrifice."

Vocation

To know your vocation: "(1) Ask God in prayer; (2) ask one's spiritual director; (3) ask oneself, knowing one's own inclinations."

"Everything has a particular end and obeys a law. Everything develops toward a predestined end. God has traced a way for each one of us. . . . Both our earthly and eternal happiness depends on following our vocation very carefully."

"Every vocation is a call to motherhood or fatherhood, earthly, spiritual, and moral. God has placed in us an instinct for life. A priest is a father, nuns are mothers, mothers of souls."

"Woe to those young people who do not accept the vocation of motherhood."

"Each of us must prepare ourselves for our own vocation and prepare ourselves to be givers of life."

"All the Lord's ways are beautiful because their end is one and the same: to save our own soul and to succeed in leading many other souls to heaven, to give glory to God."

"If during the struggles to carry out our vocation, we should have to die, that would be the most beautiful day of our life."

Love

"To love means the desire to perfect oneself and the loved one, to overcome selfishness and to give oneself."

"Love must be total, full, complete, governed by God's law and it must carry over into eternity."

PHOTOGRAPHIC CREDITS

The photographs of Saint Gianna Molla and family were supplied courtesy of the Society of Saint Gianna Beretta Molla, Philadelphia, Pennsylvania.

The photograph of Saint Gianna's office on page 76 was supplied courtesy of Nellie Boldrick.